Rugby Training

RUGBY Training

> **INCLUDES 100 PRACTICE DRILLS**

Stuart Biddle
Barrie Corless
Anne de Looy
Peter Thomas

The Crowood Press

First published in 1989 by
The Crowood Press Ltd
Ramsbury, Marlborough
Wiltshire SN8 2HR

www.crowood.com

New edition 1995

This impression 2005

British Library Cataloguing-in-Publication Data
A catalogue record for this book is available from the British Library.

ISBN 1 85223 897 6

Acknowledgements
Line illustrations for Chapter 1 by Vanetta Joffe

Typeset by Acuté, Stroud

Printed and bound in Great Britain by J. W. Arrowsmith, Bristol

Contents

THE AUTHORS

Dr STUART BIDDLE: Stuart is a senior lecturer in the School of Education, University of Exeter, where he is the course director of the MSc degree in Exercise and Sport Psychology and president of the European Federation of Sport Psychology. He is an active consultant in sport and exercise and was formerly an international weightlifting competitor and coach.

BARRIE CORLESS: Barrie had a distinguished Rugby career for Birmingham, Coventry, Moseley and England, and was the administrator for Northampton Football Club. He is now Director of Rugby at Gloucester RFC. He has extensive experience at home and abroad and has produced a coaching video for the Rugby Football Union as well as publishing *Rugby Union: The Skills of the Game* (The Crowood Press, 1985 and 1993).

Dr ANNE DE LOOY: Anne is head of Dietetics and Nutrition at Queen Margaret College, Edinburgh, and tutor to the National Coaching Foundation on sports nutrition.

Dr PETER THOMAS: Peter is a sports physician in Reading and was an Olympic oarsman in the Mexico Games of 1968. He was then the Great Britain rowing team doctor and is currently the medical director of Reading Sports Injury Clinic and a medical officer at the British Olympic Association's Medical Centre at Northwick Park.

Introduction

Rugby Union may not have achieved the world-wide popularity of some team games such as volleyball or soccer, but it remains at the forefront of British sporting interest and popularity. In some areas, such as South Wales, its popularity far exceeds other sports. In England, a healthy increase in membership of affiliated school clubs suggests that future participation rates may also rise. Indeed, the number of clubs affiliated to the Rugby Football Union (RFU) has increased steadily in recent years.

People play sport for a variety of reasons, ranging from having fun, to health and fitness, competition, making friends, skill development and others. Whatever the main reason for playing Rugby, it is likely that all players wish to improve or maintain their playing skills, including physical fitness. This involves preparing well for matches so that enjoyment is maximised.

For Rugby players seeking to achieve the highest honours, or simply to play to the very best of their ability, it is essential to have a well-planned training programme. The purpose of this book is to outline some of the fundamentals of such a training programme from which players of all levels will benefit. However, whereas most sports books – for reasons of space – concentrate on the technical and tactical skills of the game, this book aims to provide a more complete picture of the training process by looking at:

(i)   Rugby practices
(ii)   physical fitness
(iii)   nutrition
(iv)   injury prevention
(v)   mental training

This all-round approach is recommended as the best way of preparing yourself for the game of Rugby Union. Certainly at the top level of Rugby some national teams seem to be developing skills and fitness far in excess of their rivals. Perhaps this is the time to strive to improve your game by adopting the approach advocated here.

Note: the first chapter of this book presents a hundred skills practices, many of which are illustrated by line-drawings. To help you use these drawings, there is a basic key reproduced on the following page.

KEY

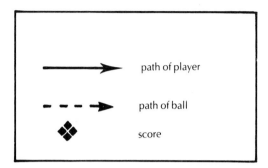

Throughout Chapter 1 the arrows and symbols shown in the key are used to denote the paths of player and ball and when a player should run on to 'score' a try.

1 Skills Practices

HANDLING

Rugby football is essentially a handling game. It is therefore of vital importance that a great deal of time is spent on this aspect of the game. With players of any age, shuttle-handling drills can be an enjoyable part of the warm-up in which players prepare for more vigorous work by handling the ball a great many times.

Drills in Threes

(1) Players move back and forth between lines about 10m apart. The ball must travel from A to C or from C to A on each length. More experienced players should be able to get the ball back to the start on each length (A to B to C to B to A).

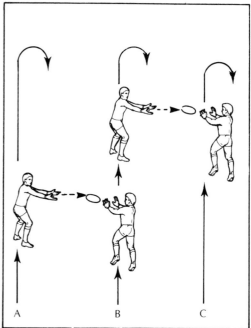

Drill 2

(2) Players run and pass. On receiving the ball, C immediately turns and runs in the opposite direction before passing to B; A, on receiving the ball, does the same. These drills work equally well with four players (two working in the middle). A rest period as well as regular changes of position are important.

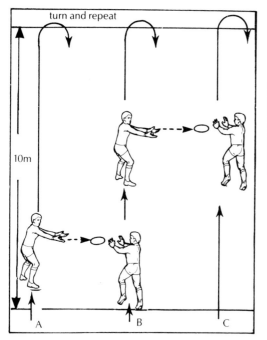

Drill 1

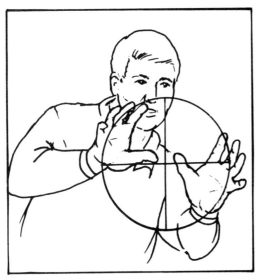

Diagram A

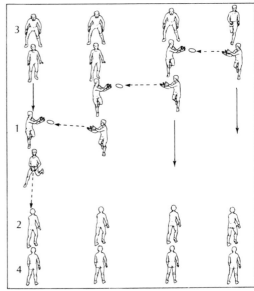

Drill 3

Coaching Points (Diagram A)

(i)   Hold up your hands to provide a target for the passer.

(ii)   Run straight.

Drill in Larger Groups

(3)   Group 1 move forward and pass the ball along the line. As soon as the end player receives the ball it is passed to the end player in group 2, who repeat the drill in the opposite direction, followed by group 3 and then group 4. After completing their length, the group moves to the rear, ready to take their next turn. Regularly change the positions of the players. As the groups become more competent, the distance between groups can be decreased thus making each group pass the ball more quickly.

(4)   Using the same formation as in the previous drill, a number of handling variations can be introduced, such as the miss pass. The first passer misses out the player next to him and passes to player C.

(5)   Miss and loop. As in the previous drill, but the player who is missed out loops to receive a pass.

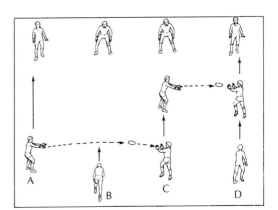

Drill 4

Coaching Points (Diagram B)

(i)   The player giving the pass (who passes to the player missed out) should turn in slightly to clear the way for the looping player.

(ii)   The player receiving the pass must run straight.

(6)   Pass and loop. The first player only passes and loops outside the receiver to take a return pass.

Drill 5a

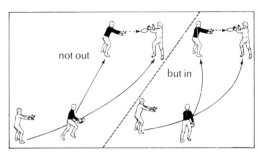

Diagram B

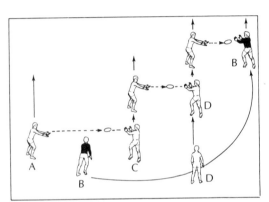

Drill 5b

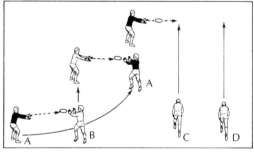

Drill 6

Coaching Points (Diagram C)

(i) As in the previous drill; allow room for the looping player and run straight.

(ii) Players C and D drift out slightly to make space for the looping A.

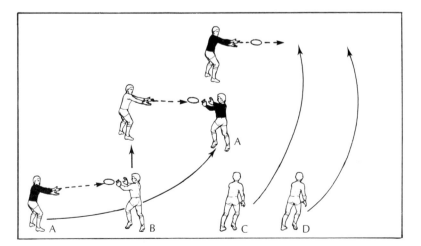

Diagram C

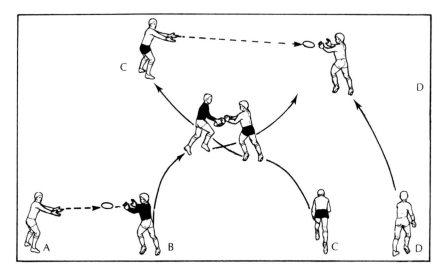

Drill 7

(7) Pass and scissors-pass. A passes to B who executes a switch or 'scissors' movement with C who passes to D to complete the drill.

(8) Continuous passing. The two middle players work continuously while the end players change after each length. Change positions regularly.

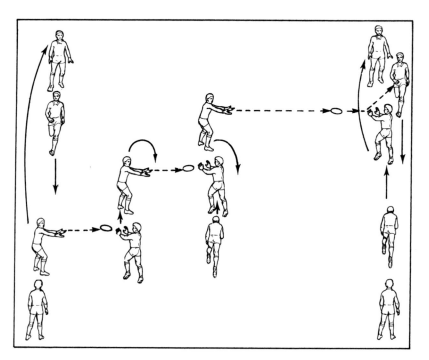

Drill 8

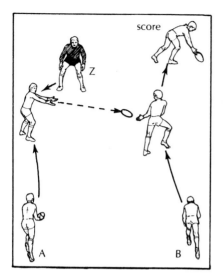

Drill 9

Two against One Drills

(9) A runs forward at speed and commits the defender to create the overlap for B. Initially defender (Z) marks A only.

(10) When technique improves, allow Z to move towards A or B.

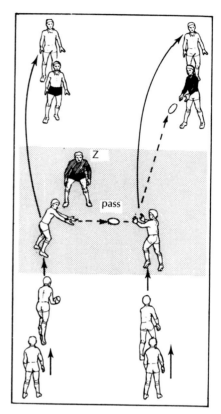

Drill 11

(11) Continuous two against one. Defender Z moves in front of the player in possession of the ball, whoever that may be – A, then B and so on. Change defender when each group has gone.

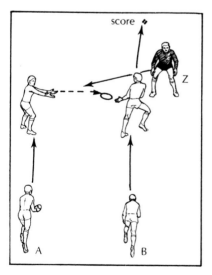

Drill 10

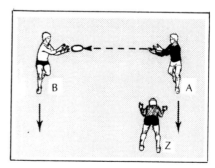

Diagram D

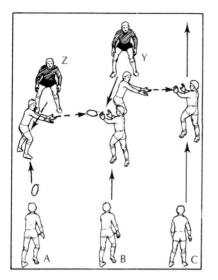

Drill 12

Coaching Points (Diagram D)

(i)   Run at speed to commit the defender.
(ii)   If there is no defender in front, run to score.
(iii)   As the defender approaches, time the pass to allow B to score.

Drill 13

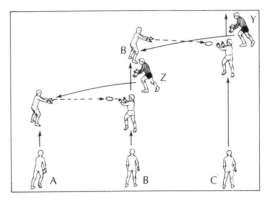

Drill 14

Three Against Two Drills

(12)   When A picks up the ball from the ground, Z moves forward, when B catches the ball, Y moves forward. In the early stages of this practice we are still creating two against one situations.

(13)   Defenders move as in (12) above, but they may also vary their position, Y covering both B and C. Coaching points are for the two-against-one exercise.

(14)   A further possibility of this situation in which defenders vary their positions is shown in the illustration.

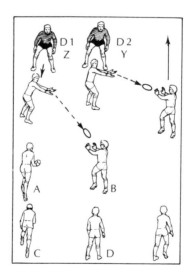

Drill 15

(15)   Continuous three against two. Defenders change after each drill – A and B change with Z and Y to be followed by C and D.

Support Play Drills

(16)   Players stand in single file – the person in possession of the ball then runs forward

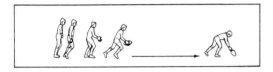

Drill 16

approximately 5m and puts the ball on the ground. The next player picks it up, runs 5m and repeats the drill.

(17)   Players stand in single file. The first player puts the ball down, the second steps over the ball and passes to the third who takes a flat pass at speed.

(18)   Players stand in single file. After putting the ball on the ground, the first player (Z) stands behind the ball as a defender. Player A steps over the ball, picks it up and commits Z before passing to B who takes the ball flat and at speed. (If the defender is close to the ball A merely picks the ball up and passes. If the defender is some distance behind the ball

Drill 17

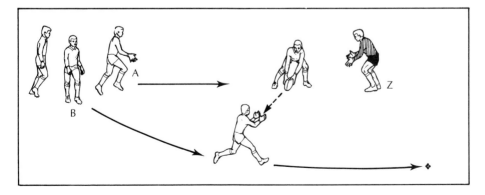

Drill 18

Drill 19

Drill 20

A must carry the ball forward to commit the defender before passing.)

(19) Two players defend, one behind the other. As the attackers approach, the rear defender moves to one side, the attackers react by attacking the free side.

(20) As in the previous drill but defender Y, after defending the space, moves across to stop B from scoring.

Continuous Loop Drills

Players work in a narrow (15m wide) channel to begin with. As expertise increases, work in channels of 10m and finally 5m.

(21) Starting in single file, players pass flat to the person behind who takes the ball on the burst. Players must stay within the channel by running straight. Alternate the direction of the pass – one length pass left to right, and then pass right to left for the next length.

short flat passes

15m

Drill 21

Drill 22

Drill 23

(22)   Players work as in the previous drill, but every pass goes in the opposite direction to the one preceding it, so that the first pass is from left to right, the next from right to left, the third from left to right and so on.

(23)   To encourage quick reactions in support and variations in support-running lines, the direction of the pass can be changed – two passes left to right, one pass right to left, followed by two more left to right and so on.

Line Through Line Drill

(24)   Two groups of players line up four, five or six abreast, one line behind the other. Both groups run forward – the front group pass the ball along the line and when the ball reaches the end player, the second line sprint to the front and repeat the drill.

Continuous Passing Drills

(25)   Four pairs of players line up holding a ball – the distance apart depends upon the ability of the passers (young players 10m apart, senior players 5m apart is a rough guide). Player 1 receives a pass from players A, B, C and D in turn. In each case he then turns and passes to the free catcher, players E, F, G or H.

(26)   This drill can also be used with two or three players running and passing.

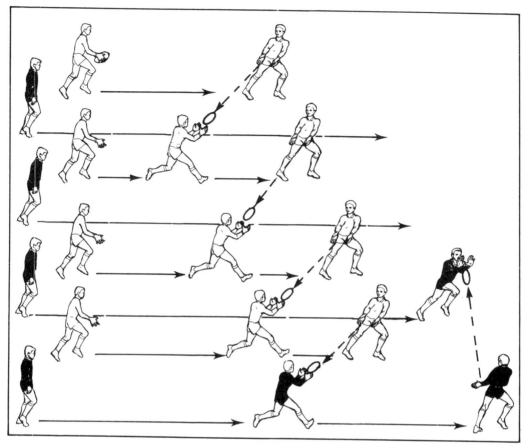

Drill 24

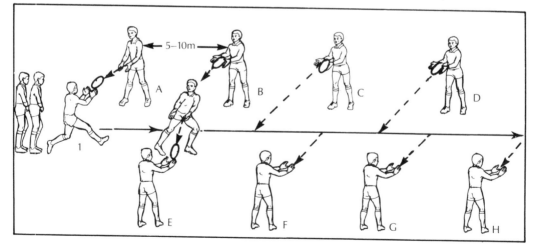

Drill 25

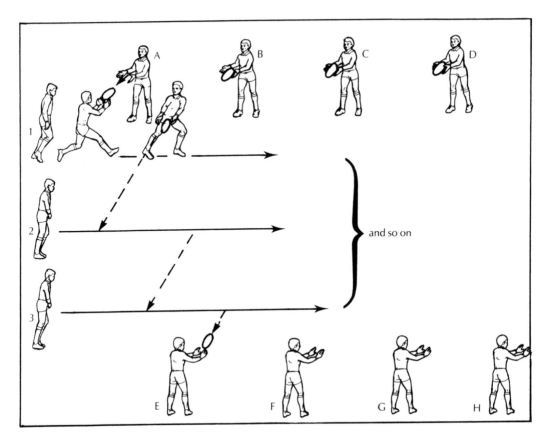

Drill 26

Continuous Passing Drill

(27)   Here players are passing across a grid. B receives a pass from A, then passes to C, who passes to D. B and C run to the far side of the grid, then turn and repeat.

Slip Catching Drill

(28)   It is necessary from time to time to rest and recover from strenuous bouts of activity. While resting players can use this time to improve their handling dexterity. Players stand in a circle, passing the ball round the group. On the command 'change' the passing goes in the opposite direction.

(29)   There are a number of variations on drill 28 which may be tried, such as passing above the waist, below the knees, passing the ball from hand to hand round the body and then to the next player or passing the ball in a figure of eight through the legs and then on to the next player.

Coaching Point

The receiver should reach towards the ball, swing it across the body and use the wrists to direct the pass onwards.

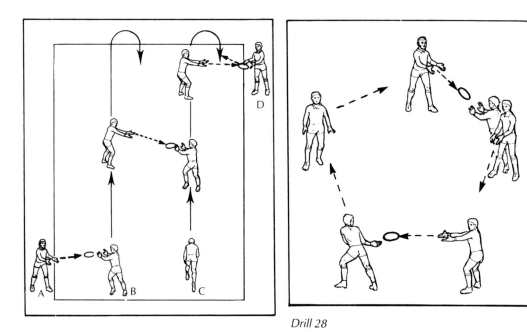

Drill 27

Drill 28

Drill 30

Give and Go Drill

(30) Two files of players line up facing each other. The front player of one file has the ball and passes it to the opposite player. The passer then runs to the rear of the opposite file. The person now in possession of the ball repeats the drill and so on.

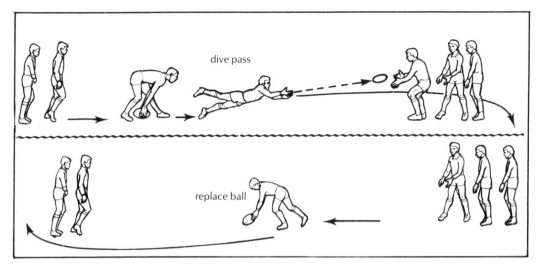

Drill 31

(31)   Players line up as in drill 30 with the ball on the ground between the files. The front player runs to the ball, executes a dive pass, gets up and runs to the rear of the opposite file. The player catching the ball puts it down between the files and runs to the rear of the opposite file.

(32)   As drill 31, but the lead player passes the ball from the ground while still standing.

(33)   The front player carries the ball, throws it into the air, jumps to catch it with both feet off the ground and hands above head, and on landing passes to the front player in the next group who repeats.

(34)   The ball is placed on the ground between the groups. The front player picks it up and places it in front of the facing group. The other front player repeats.

Coaching Point

The rear foot should be near the ball and the leading foot should point towards the target. There should be no backswing on the pass.

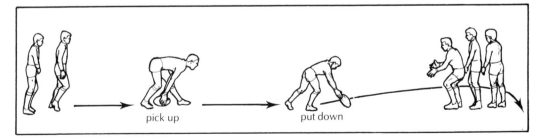

Drill 34

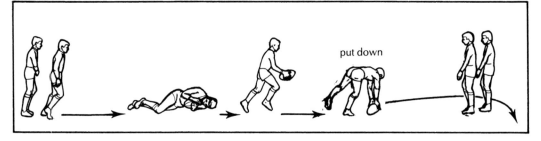

Drill 35

(35) As for drill 34, but the player falls on the ball, gets up quickly and then places it in front of the opposite group who repeat the exercise.

(37) As in drill 36, except that each group has a ball and shuttles backwards and forwards across a 15m area, always controlling the ball and avoiding the opposition.

Pass and Evade Drill

(36) Four groups of four players each line up. The front two groups each carry a ball and move towards each other, passing the ball down the line. As they cross, players avoid each other and ensure the passes are not blocked. The drill is repeated with the next two (or more) groups.

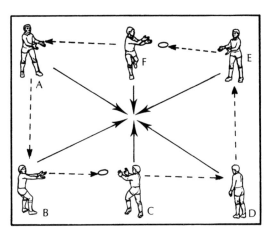

Drill 38

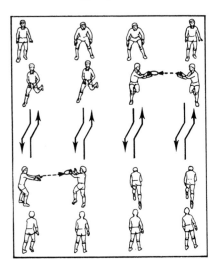

Drill 36

(38) Two groups of three line up facing each other 5m apart. Two players at opposite corners have a ball, both of which are passed around the outside of the rectangle from player to player. As soon as they have passed the ball, the players change positions so that A and D, B and E and C and F all swap positions. Players must pass the ball before they run and must be careful to avoid collisions and to watch the ball at all times.

Drill 39

Straighten Line and Pass Drills

These are practices to encourage straight running, which commits the defenders and maintains space outside for the overlapping player to exploit.

(39)   Players are encouraged to run towards the inside shoulder of an imaginary defender before passing back inside. This can be practised by players running towards the touch-line and then passing back inside to a supporting player.

(40)   Supporting players should be encouraged to run straight *before* they receive the ball. This can be practised using drill 39, making sure that players run straight before taking the ball.

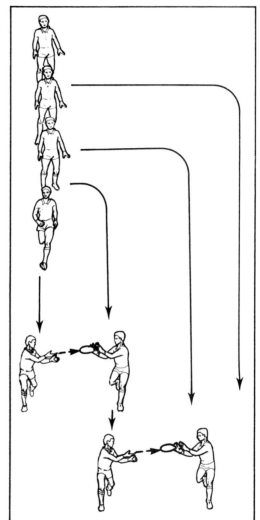

Drill 40

(41)   Again, drill 39 can be adapted so that a two-against-one situation is produced. For this practice, the ball carrier should run inwards before passing to a supporting player.

(42)   Drill 39 may be changed to create a three-against-two situation. It is important that players turn inwards before passing, and that support players run straight before receiving the ball.

Drill 41

Drill 43

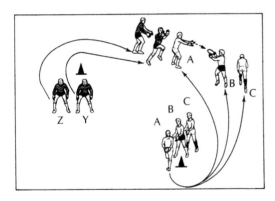

Drill 42

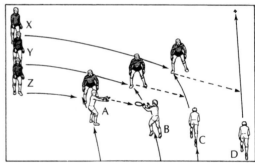

Drill 44

(43) Four against three. Each player in turn runs towards the inside shoulder of the defender opposite and then passes the ball. Players should be on the correct line, running at speed to prevent the defender drifting sideways to cut off the overlap.

(44) For this drill, defenders approach from the side. The ball carrier once again runs at the inside shoulder to commit the defender and prevent a drift toward the touch-line. Initially defenders do not move until the player they are marking has the ball. As the drill progresses the defenders should begin to move earlier.

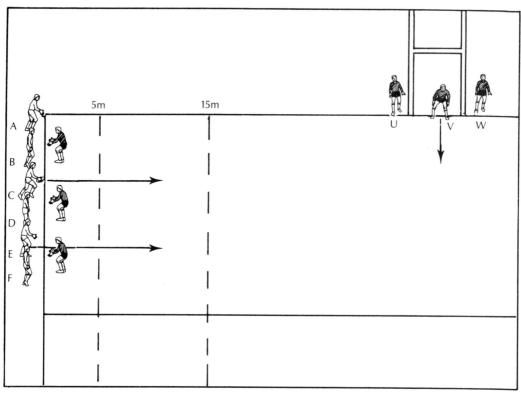

Drill 45

(45) The next stage is to test the players' ability in fully-opposed situations across the pitch. The attackers are confronted by three defenders in the 5m area who can move forwards or sideways but *not* backwards. When attackers cross the 15m line, a second wave of three defenders approach from the side. Using the technique practised above, the attackers move across the pitch to score.

RUNNING SKILLS

Many running skills associated with Rugby football can be improved by incorporating them in a series of relays and games.

(46) The player runs, picks the ball up at 1, weaves in and out of the cones, places the ball at 2, runs round the last post, picks the ball up again, weaves back through the cones, places ball at 1. The next player starts to run as soon as the ball is replaced at 1. The ball must be carried in both hands at all times.

(47) Players line up in two groups of three at start 1 and start 2. The first player from start 1 runs round cone A to cone B, zigzags up and back, on to cone C and then to start 2. The first player from start 2 does the exercise in reverse. As players reach the 'opposite' start, their team-mate sets off.

(48) Corner Spry. The first player A gives and receives a pass from team-mates B, C, D, E and F. On receiving the final pass from B player A places the ball on the ground, runs round the team and outside the grid. Meanwhile B has moved to pick up the ball, the other players move across and A returns to position F and receives the first pass from B. The first team to their original position wins.

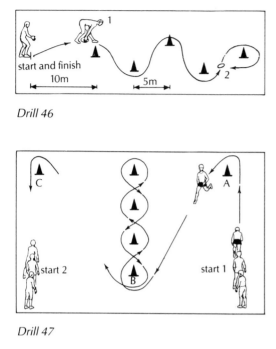

Drill 46

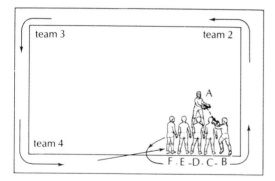

Drill 47

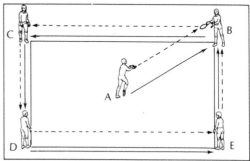

Drill 49

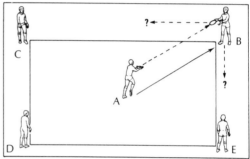

Drill 50

Drill 48

Catch Ball Drill

(50) Starting position as for drill 49. This time A chases the ball round the grid, attempting to catch any player in possession. Players B, C, D and E may pass the ball in any direction round the square. Player A works for perhaps twenty seconds and then changes places with a player outside the square.

Give and Go Drill

(49) Each player stands at one corner of a grid square with a fifth player (A) holding the ball in the middle of the grid. A passes the ball to the nearest corner and follows the pass. Player B catches and passes to C and follows the pass. The drill is repeated until the players return to their starting positions.

Criss Cross Drills

(51) This is a very intensive running and handling drill with simple beginnings. Players line up with the ball at two opposite corners of a rectangle. They start by passing the balls to the left, both at the same time. After they have passed the ball the corner players A and D change places; next the middle players C and F change places after they have

27

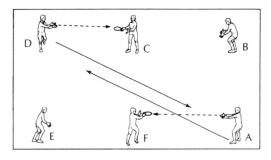

Drill 51

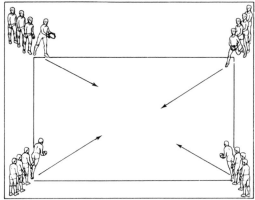

Drill 53

passed, and then finally B and E change places. Remember to think ahead, pass before running and keep your eyes open!

(52)   Tag. Six players in a grid, one holding the ball. Moving anywhere in the grid, the five players try to keep away from the ball carrier – who attempts to touch them with the ball while holding it in two hands. When caught, the chaser and the caught player change roles.

Grid Cross Over Running Drills

(53)   Four players line up at each corner of a grid, with the front player holding the ball. The first four players from each corner run diagonally across the square keeping the ball in both hands and avoiding any contact. Hand balls to next four players who repeat the exercise.

(54)   Players line up as in drill 53. This time the four players holding the ball run to any corner but no two players should arrive at the same corner together. Each player must find a spare player to pass to.

(55)   The same starting position as for drill 53, except that a ball is placed on the ground in front of each group. The four front players pick up the balls and, avoiding any contact, run diagonally across the grid and place the ball in front of the opposite group.

(56)   Begin as for drill 53, but this time the four front players run across the grid and pick up the far ball, pass it to the front player who places it on the ground, runs across the grid to pick up the far ball and so on.

(57)   The exercise is broadly the same as drill 56, but players fall on the far ball, regain their feet and give the ball to a front player who replaces it and repeats the exercise with the far ball.

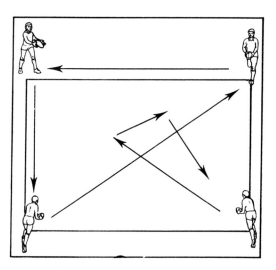

Drill 54

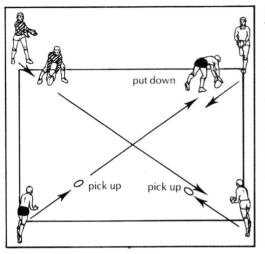

Drill 55

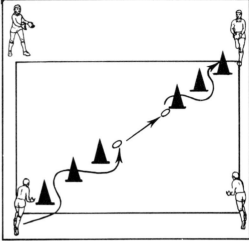

Drill 58

Drill 56

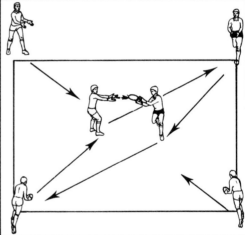

Drill 59

(58) Place three cones in front of each group. Players swerve between the cones, pick up the ball and put it down before reaching the opposite set of cones through which they zigzag before joining the back of the opposite group.

(59) This exercise uses two balls, one for each pair of diagonally-opposite groups. As the players converge in the centre of the grid, the ball carrier passes to his opposite player. The players continue across the grid when the next four players repeat the exercise.

(60) Two balls are placed on the ground between the diagonally-opposite groups. Player A picks up the ball and passes to B, who immediately places the ball on the ground. (C and D are also working at the

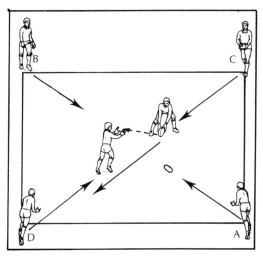

Drill 60

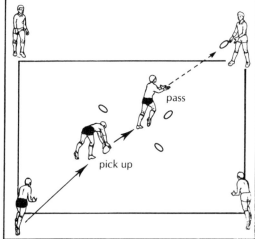

Drill 61

same time.) As soon as the ball is placed on the ground, the next group begins.

(61)   Four balls are placed on the ground in the centre of the grid. The first four players run out, pick up their ball and pass it to the player diagonally opposite. The next four players run out and replace the balls and continue across the grid, the next four pick up and pass, and so on.

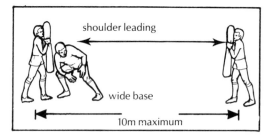

Drill 62

CONTACT PRACTICES

Contact practices should be designed in such a way as to produce good technique, and be safe and enjoyable in order to develop the players' confidence. The players should be kept alert at all times and younger players should not approach contact situations too quickly: slowly and with control is the rule.

Contact-Pad Drills

(62)   In turn, players shuttle between the pads: carrying a ball, they bump the pad staying balanced and on their feet (which should be spread wide apart on contact), shoulders leaning into the pad. *Note:* if the pad is taken away, the driving player should *not* fall over.

(63)   Players work in pairs, with the ball carrier bumping into the pad and passing to the partner, who runs around the 'pad-holder' and drives into the opposite players.

(64)   As contact is made with the pad, the ball carrier places the ball on the ground and drives past the ball. The player then picks up the ball and repeats on the second pad.

(65)   The ball carrier drives into the contact pad and presents the ball to the support player by holding it in the arm furthest away from the pad. The body acts as a screen to prevent the opposition from gaining possession. The

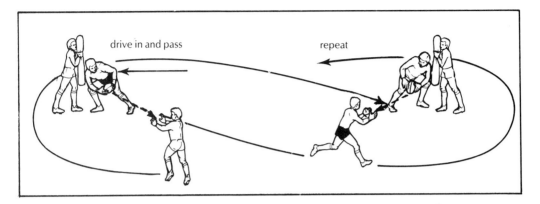

Drill 63

Drill 64

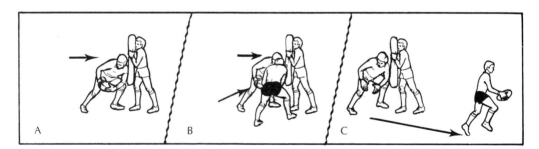

Drill 65

support player then drives in for two reasons: to protect the ball by leading with the opposite shoulder to the ball carrier and to sustain the forward drive provided by the ball carrier. The two players – in a V-formation around the ball – continue driving until the second player emerges with the ball.

31

Drill 66

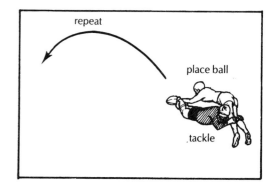

Drill 68

(66)   This exercise uses the same technique as drill 64, but this time, as the second player emerges with the ball, a pass is made to a support player who is running at full speed.

Coaching Points

(i)   All players should adopt a low body-position two or three strides before contact.
(ii)   Players should bend at the knees and drive upwards to stay on their feet.
(iii)   An arm should be used for additional stability if required by binding onto an opponent or a team-mate.

TACKLING

(67)   The tacklers form a semi-circle and are on their knees. The ball carriers run at the outside shoulder of the tackler and pass the ball back inside after the tackle.

(68)   As drill 67, except that players imagine there is no-one available to receive the pass so as they are tackled they *place* the ball on the ground. The next player picks it up and repeats. (The ball must be placed under control away from the body so that it is easily available for the support player.)

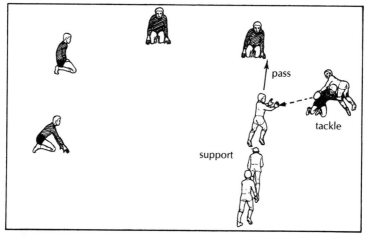

Drill 67

Drill 69

(69)   As drill 68, except that the next (support) player steps over the ball to provide protection against the opposition for both ball and player. The ball is then picked up and passed to a support player, who drives into the next tackler.

(70)   To bring an element of decision-making to the practice, the ball carrier either passes or places the ball on the floor and the supporting player either picks up and drives on or steps over the ball and then passes it. Each player must, of course, react to the decision made by the player in front.

The following drills may be converted into small-side games.

(71)   Two against two. Play is from the touchline to the 15m line. The first defender stands inside the 5m channel and the second stands in the 5m–15m channel. The first attacking player tries to beat the defender in front –

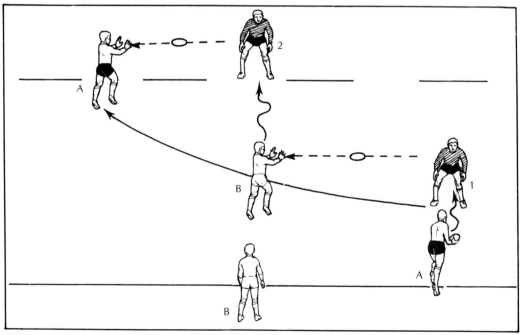

Drill 71

when tackled, the attacker passes to a support player or places the ball on the ground. The second attacker catches or picks up the ball and tries to beat the second defender. When tackled, the second attacker passes to the first attacker who must be ready in support.

(72)   Expand this to a three against three situation; all the attacking players must regain their feet and also handle the ball after the third tackle.

(73)   As in the previous drill, except that all the attackers and the defenders regain their feet and handle the ball after the third tackle.

(74)   Three against three. Allow the defenders to retreat and continue to tackle across the width of the pitch.

CONTINUITY IN CONTACT

Having won the ball from a set piece, the aim must be to prevent the opposition from winning it back. This depends on good support (fitness) and the ability of the ball carrier to present the ball correctly on contact.

(75)   Moving down a narrow channel 10m wide, groups of four players are confronted by four defenders spaced 10m apart. Moving the defender by taking the correct running line and passing the ball early will allow the four attacking players to score at the end of the channel.

(76)   Vary the size of the channel – 10m or 15m at the start and 5m at finish, for example – and alter the number and position of the defenders to pose a different problem for the attackers.

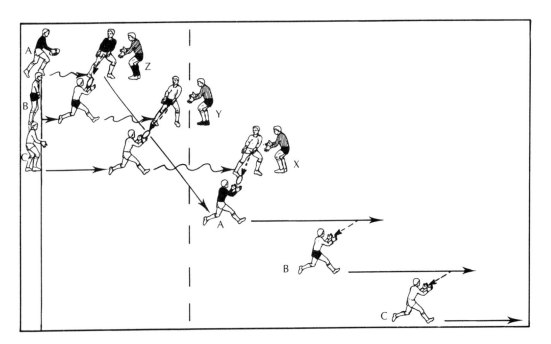

Drill 72

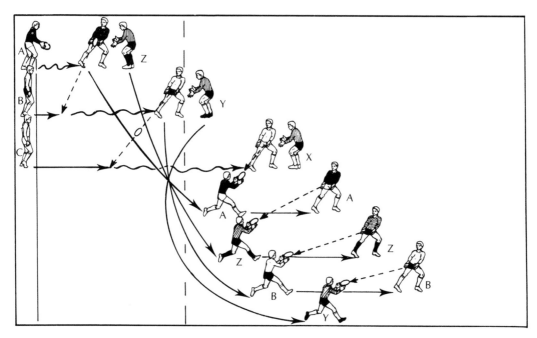

Drill 73

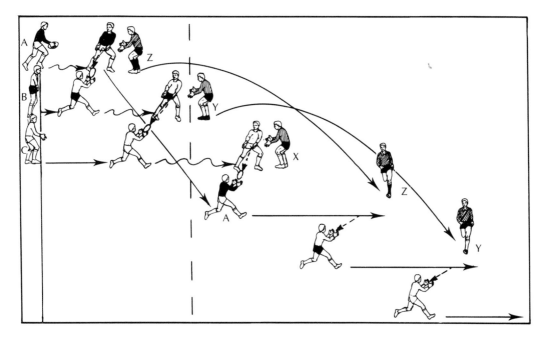

Drill 74

(77) Assume that the ball cannot be passed before contact is made. The ball carrier should therefore execute a screen pass to a support player as follows: take a long stride 'into contact', leading with the shoulder and hip – this turns the body as a shield to protect the ball. The ball is kept close to the body as contact is made, then either held for the support to take or 'popped' in the air for support to run on to.

(78) If the opposition manage to prevent the delivery of a screen pass it may be necessary for the support player to drive in to move the ball away from the ball carrier. The ball carrier drives into contact as before (a long stride, shoulder and hip leading, ball protected) and the support player drives in with the *opposite* shoulder, so protecting the ball completely from the opposition. Once the ball carrier has secured the ball, the support player can take it and drive away into space.

(79) If it is not possible or desirable to drive on with the ball, the support player can pass to the next supporting player, so putting speed back into the movement and maintaining continuity.

Coaching Point

The importance of a good body position in all situations concerned with contact and close driving support should be emphasised. Players should be low but always in a position to stay on their feet.

(80) The development of a *maul* from this exercise is quite straightforward. The ball carrier makes contact and presents the ball as before. The first support player leads with the opposite shoulder, secures the ball and continues the forward drive. The next two supporting players bind on these players with their inside arm while still driving forward. They may use their outside arm to bind in any close opponents. While the maul is secure and moving forward, the second

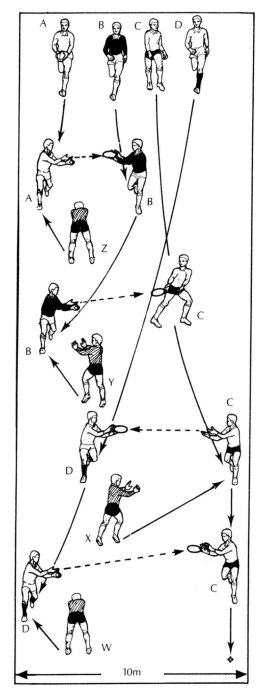

Drill 75

Drill 76

Drill 77

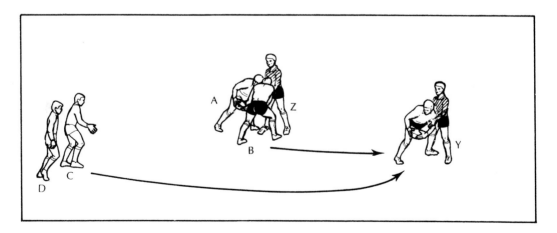

Drill 78

Drill 80

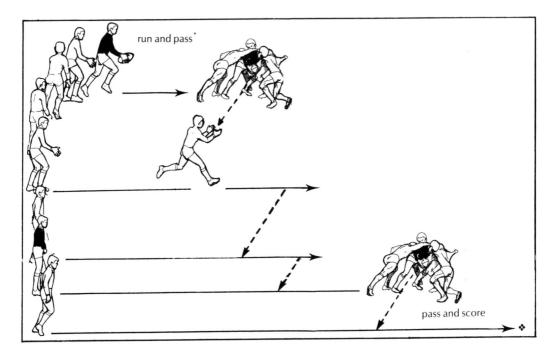

Drill 82

player takes the ball and passes it to the scrum-half. (It is important that the ball is presented *before* the maul stops moving.)

(81)   To convert this into a *ruck* the role of all the support players stays the same, the only difference being that the ball is placed on the ground either by the player securing the ball or the player going to ground and placing the ball for the scrum-half. In each case the rest of the players continue the forward drive until the ball is clear.

(82)   The two previous drills can be put into a small game situation. The ball is presented from a ruck or maul to the scrum-half who passes it to a small group of three-quarters. They run and pass until they meet the next line of defenders. The ball is presented and supported as before by the nearest players (who may be forwards or backs). Once the ball has been won for the second time, it is passed until a try is scored – the whole exercise taking 25m.

SOME CONTACT IDEAS FOR YOUNG PLAYERS

In order to develop strength and confidence in younger players, it is a good idea to provide some activities of a competitive nature which

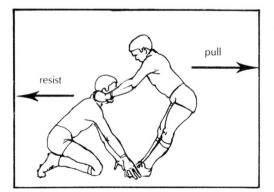

Drill 83

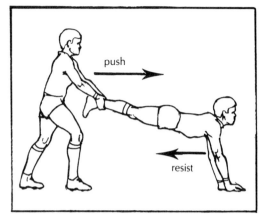

Drill 84

will physically tax the players and improve techniques (*see* Chapter 2 for additional material on strength development). Here are some examples:

(83)   Stubborn mule. One player kneels and places both hands on the ground. With hands clasped behind the kneeling player's neck, the partner pulls, attempting to move the kneeling player. The kneeling player resists, keeping chin up and neck rigid to resist the pull. Change position as soon as the kneeling player moves.

(84)   Obstinate wheelbarrow. Two players take positions as if taking part in a 'wheelbarrow' race: however, the 'barrow' does not move the hands; by keeping the chin up, arms and back straight, the player resists the partner's push. Change positions once the barrow moves.

(85)   Lift and turn. Four players stand one in each corner of a grid looking out. One player in the grid runs to each corner in turn and, gripping the corner player firmly around the waist and using the *legs*, lifts and turns so that the corner player faces the centre of the grid. It is important to use the legs, rather than the back, to lift.

(86)   Wrestle ball. The players are positioned as in drill 85, but the centre player

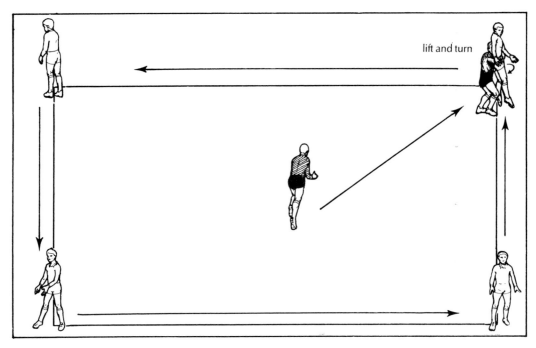

Drill 85

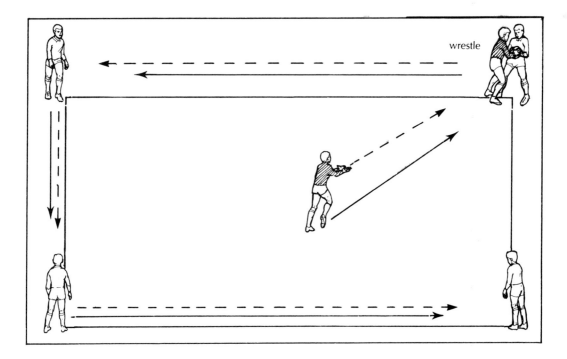

Drill 86

Drill 87

Drill 88

has a ball. The ball is passed to the player in one corner who grips it firmly. The passer then attempts to wrestle the ball free. If the passer is still unsuccessful after five seconds, the holder releases the ball which is passed to the next corner and the drill is repeated.

(87) Turn and wrestle. By combining the two previous activities a small game can be played in the grid. The ball is passed to any player who turns back on to the opposing players and grips the ball tightly. The nearest opposing player turns the ball carrier who is then held exposed to the other players. The next nearest player rips the ball away and passes it to a spare player who moves to a space, turns back on and the drill is repeated.

(88) Close contact end ball – two against two or three against three. A player from each team takes up a stationary position at each end of the grid. The other players stand in the centre of the grid facing their 'goalkeeper'. The game is started by throwing the ball in the air between the players. On gaining possession, a player tries to evade the opponent and hand the ball to the goalkeeper (a try). If held or put to the floor, the ball must be released to the opposing player. Play restarts after a try by the goalkeeper handing the ball to the opposing player. Play is continuous. This is an extremely tiring game and frequent changes of position are necessary. In a three against three game the players are allowed to pass the ball to each other in any direction (all other rules are the same).

(89) Roll and fall. Players work in pairs, one standing with legs apart. The player's partner rolls the ball through the standing player's legs, runs round the player and falls on the ball. The partner immediately gets up and then repeats the exercise in the opposite direction.

(90) The same drill as 89, except that the standing player turns and moves to oppose

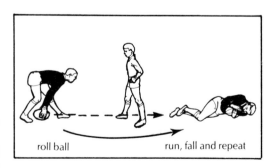

Drill 89

Drill 91

the player who is getting up after falling on the ball. It is essential that players regain their feet as soon as possible and have a good body position on contact.

(91) Add an extra attacking player who follows the 'faller' and moves in to secure the ball and drive forward with it.

IMPROVING KICKING

Much of the kicking we see in matches is aimless and adds very little to constructive team play. This may be because very little kicking practice directly relevant to game situations is practised by most players. The following should help improve your kicking.

(92) Punting. Two or four players face each other, holding a ball 5–10m apart. Gently kick the ball to your partner(s), experimenting with a variety of kicks (high chip, low screw kick and so on), always concentrating on accuracy. When confident, stand further apart and repeat the exercise. It is important to develop confidence in the use of both left and right feet.

(93) Chip and catch. The ball carrier runs towards the goal-posts, kicks the ball over the crossbar, and runs between the posts to catch the ball before it touches the ground.

(94) Chip, catch and evade. As drill 93,

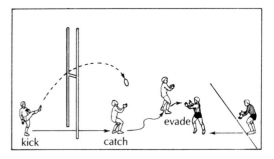

Drill 94

except that the kicker evades a defender before scoring on the 22m line. The defender stands on the 22m line and does not move until the kicker has caught the ball.

(95) Grubber-kick. Players 'grub-kick' the ball along the ground between two marker cones, gather the ball and score a try. Vary the space between the cones and grub-kick with the instep and with the top of the foot (for the ball to run further ahead). An accurate kick which can be gathered by the kicker should always be the aim.

(96) Grub-kick the ball into a target area for a second player to follow up and score. This demands accuracy of placement when kicking and also the correct weight to ensure the ball stays in the target area.

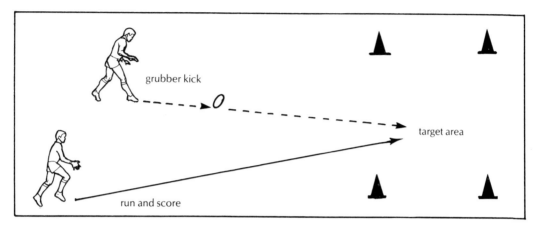

Drill 96

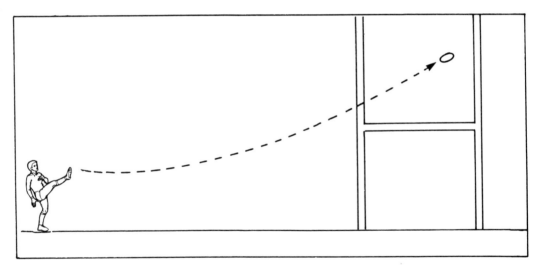

Drill 99

(97) Kicking against defenders. You can play two against one or two against two; the ball carrier uses a variety of kicks to enable the partner to gather the ball and score.

(98) Kicks to touch. Practise screw-kicks into touch with the right foot to the left hand touch-line and vice versa. Practise standing on the touch-line to screw-kick the ball along and over the line, then move to the 5m and 15m lines on each side of the field, judging the kick as precisely as possible each time.

(99) To improve the accuracy of your screw-kicking, a good practice is to try to kick the ball between the goal-posts from a position on the goal line so that you must 'bend' the ball with great accuracy.

(100) When outside your own 22m area, kicks may not go into touch without bouncing. Practices which aim to bounce the ball before crossing the touch-line are important.

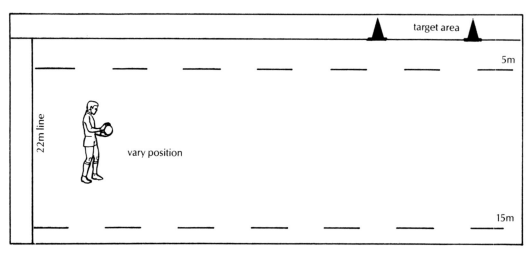

Drill 100

Place two markers on the touch-line to improve accuracy and, once again, practise from various positions in the field of play. All of these exercises should be practised with opponents in order to speed up the players' reactions. The kicker catches the ball and either kicks to touch before the opponent arrives or evades the defender and then finds touch.

2   Physical Fitness

The constant rise in standards in sport can be attributed to many things, such as improved techniques and equipment. What heights, for example, would pole-vaulters be managing without fibre-glass poles? However, in some sports the equipment is relatively unimportant and the techniques may not have changed much. What then can account for improvements in these sports? Quite probably the key factor is *physical fitness*. However much it actually contributes to the end result in Rugby, it is now recognised that fitness is a very important part of training. Indeed fitness is important in all levels of the game for while it is essential for international competition, it is also beneficial for beginners, improving both their effectiveness and enjoyment of the game.

WHAT IS PHYSICAL FITNESS?

Physical fitness involves a multitude of components, thus making it difficult to identify fitness as one single thing. In fact when people ask how fit you are, they are asking a rather naive question. If I was asked the same type of question about my car, I might say that it is excellent for comfort, good on motorways, not very good for acceleration and in need of improvement when starting in the wet! An overall comment on how good (fit) my car is depends on which aspect is being referred to.

Similarly, we can refer to many different parts, or components, of fitness. Nowadays there is a great deal of interest in fitness for health, which includes exercises for stamina (such as jogging), posture, weight control and so on. However, fitness for sport will include some of these components as well as others, such as speed and power. The importance of each component for your sport obviously depends on the sport itself. Rugby is a dynamic 'all-round' game requiring most types of fitness. Nevertheless, you can imagine the marathon runner and weight-lifter having, for the most part, quite different fitness training programmes.

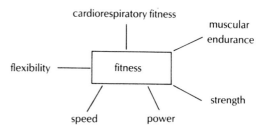

Fig 1   A model of physical fitness for sport.

The components of physical fitness for sport which require physical training are summarised in Fig 1. As you can see, these components are cardiorespiratory fitness (stamina), muscular endurance, strength, power, speed, and flexibility. Many years ago sports coaches used to refer to the main components of fitness as the 'six Ss' – stamina, strength, speed, suppleness, skill and (p)sychology! One could easily add mental fitness, diet and nutrition, injury prevention and other areas to Fig 1. However, the diagram refers to the main components of fitness which require physical activity and cause changes in the physiological state of the body.

A final point on the definition of fitness; it is sometimes claimed that fitness is a set of attributes that individuals have or achieve and which help in the ability to perform physical activity. The phrase 'have or achieve' is interesting since it suggests that sporting fitness is dependent on one or both of two factors: natural ability ('have') and training ('achieve'). Many aspects of fitness are governed by our heredity, yet with training we are able to make the most of what we have. Unfortunately, 750cc Fiats will never race in Formula One events. However, you may enjoy racing a good 750cc Fiat if it is given the right care and attention, especially if you compete against cars of the same type. Indeed, with good maintenance (training) the 750cc Fiat will be able to beat a less well maintained car with a larger engine, probably possessing other valuable qualities apart from simple power.

PRINCIPLES OF FITNESS TRAINING

Regardless of the fitness component we are talking about, certain basic principles apply to all aspects of fitness training in Rugby. These are:

(i)   frequency
(ii)   intensity
(iii)   time
(iv)   type of exercise
(v)   specificity
(vi)   reversibility
(vii)   progressive overload

Frequency

Frequency refers to the number of training sessions over a particular period of time, usually the number of sessions per week. Most sports require two or three although obviously those people striving for the highest honours will train much more frequently. (Indeed, many sports today require top

athletes to train several times a day!) However, for most people, a significant improvement in fitness can be made with three or so sessions each week.

Intensity

This refers to how hard the athlete trains. This will differ greatly between individuals, although similar training programmes can be performed on a relative basis. This means, for example, that two athletes can perform three sets of five repetitions of the leg-press exercise in the weight-training room at 75 per cent of their maximum. However, the actual weight lifted may differ considerably. Superior athletes with an extensive training background are also likely to be able to train at a higher level for longer and to recover more quickly. The intensity of the training will largely determine its effectiveness. Too little intensity will not produce much of an effect while too much intensity is likely to lead to

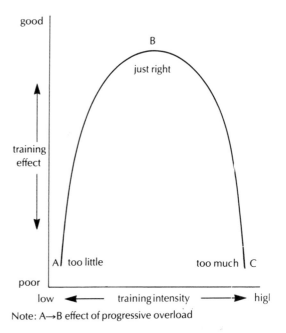

Note: A→B effect of progressive overload

Fig 2   Progressive overload.

injury and fatigue. For these reasons, the principle of *progressive overload* is important (*see* Fig 2).

Progressive Overload

The old story of Milo carrying a calf on his shoulders is the perfect illustration of progressive overload. Milo started off carrying a small calf but as the animal grew in size and weight, he did not find it progressively more difficult to carry. Instead, he adapted to the increasing load as his muscles grew stronger. Eventually, he could carry a fully-grown bull! Two things are important here: first, Milo was *progressive* in his training; he gradually adapted to the increasing load. Imagine what would have happened if he tried to lift the bull having had several months of inactivity! Second, Milo adapted to the load through *overload*. This is a fundamental mechanism since, with training, the body will either adapt and grow (with sensible progressive overload) or collapse (through inappropriate training – 'too much too soon'). This is illustrated in Fig 2.

Time

This simply refers to the amount of time spent in a training session. This will vary greatly depending on the sport and the individual, but most fitness-training sessions, allowing for adequate warm-up and cool-down, last forty minutes or more.

Type (of Exercise)

Fitness-training sessions will vary in terms of the type of exercise used. Some sessions will contain predominantly cardiorespiratory exercises, others strength and flexibility and so on. This will depend, again, on the individual and the sport in question. For example, the fitness requirements of the No. 8 will clearly differ from those of the three-quarters.

You may have noticed that the above concepts can be easily remembered by using the word FITT, the letters standing for frequency, intensity (including overload), time and type. This 'FITT principle' forms the corner-stone for many sports' fitness-training programmes. However, there are other basic principles to remember.

Specificity

Ultimately the aim of your fitness training must be to make you a better Rugby player. It may be very satisfying to improve your best lift on the bench press in the weights room, but if it does not help your Rugby it is misplaced training. Fitness training, therefore, should be specific to the sport in question – Rugby. However, this does not mean that the fundamental components of fitness are ignored. It would be pointless to train for hours every day to improve your arm strength for mauling if you lack the fundamental agility and speed to get to the maul early! A combination of exercises is therefore required.

Reversibility

'Use it or lose it!' is a common expression in sport. Unless you continue training, the fitness you have built up will quickly be lost. Some people seem to retain their fitness better than others but these individuals probably have a high natural ability to perform, as mentioned earlier. They will still lose the effects of training if they fail to continue, but the effects may not appear to be so marked. A run-down Formula One car will still beat a well-tuned 750cc Fiat!

Fitness components	Not very important	Useful	Important	Very important
Cardiorespiratory Fitness			T	BR/F
Muscular Endurance		T		BR/F
Strength			T/BR	F
Power				T/BR/F
Speed (and agility)			F	T/BR
Flexibility			T/BR/F	

T = backs (three-quarters)
BR = back-row forwards
F = forwards (front five)

Fig 3   Fitness components for Rugby.

COMPONENTS OF FITNESS FOR RUGBY

Rugby is a fast game requiring players to develop all of the qualities outlined in Fig 1. However, in Rugby some of these components are considered more important than others. Fig 3 gives a guide as to the relative importance of each of the fitness components for Rugby. The purpose of this section of the chapter, therefore, is to outline each of these components and show how they can be developed to maximise their effectiveness in Rugby. Before these components are considered, it is important to say something about the warm-up.

Warm-Up

An important part of the training process, the warm-up is a period of exercise performed before the main part of the training session or game. It is used to prepare the body for subsequent vigorous action and can be divided into two main phases: general warm-up and sport-specific warm-up.

The general warm-up should consist of two main exercises: gentle, rhythmic 'total body' exercises, such as jogging or calisthenics, which should slowly increase in intensity and produce a light sweat and raised pulse, and secondly static stretching exercises (*see* section on flexibility later in this chapter).

The sport-specific part of the warm-up, as the name suggests, should include exercises which specifically prepare you for your game, such as jumping exercises for line-out specialists, back exercises for props, wind-up sprints for wingers and so on. These can then be followed by practices of the skills themselves. The warm-up process for Rugby is summarised in Fig 4.

In addition to preparing to start activity, you should also prepare to finish! This is done by cooling-down after periods of vigorous activity using exercises similar to those for warming-up, such as gentle rhythmic exercises and stretching. In fact, this is a particularly good time for stretching as your muscles will be warm and so very receptive to this form of exercise.

CARDIORESPIRATORY FITNESS

Let us first try to understand the terminology! Cardiorespiratory (CR) fitness can also be known as cardiovascular fitness, aerobic exercise, stamina fitness and probably a host of other names. For our purposes cardiorespiratory fitness is probably good enough and it is achieved through the stamina-type exercises associated with activities such as

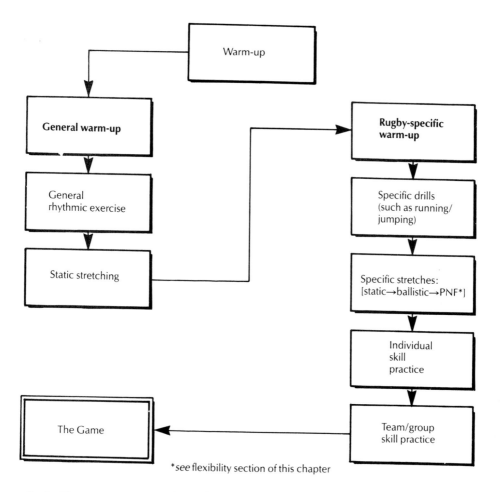

*see flexibility section of this chapter

Fig 4   The warm-up process for Rugby.

cycling, jogging and swimming. The local muscular endurance fitness needed in exercises like sit-ups or press-ups is, of course, very much related to cardiorespiratory fitness since it is the CR system that is responsible for getting oxygen to the working muscles. However, specific local muscular endurance will be considered separately since many different exercises can be prescribed for this fitness component.

Physiologists have known for a long time that the body operates through different types of energy system. For example, wingers require short bursts of high-intensity effort while forwards need more prolonged effort often at a lower intensity. The three main energy systems are summarised in Fig 5. From this you will see that CR fitness, or stamina, is associated with the aerobic energy system. The word aerobic means 'with air' (or oxygen) and is applied to continuous activities in which the oxygen that is taken in is sufficient to supply the energy required for that particular activity – so walking is aerobic and sprinting is anaerobic (without oxygen/air), as high-speed sprinting

	ENERGY SYSTEMS		
	1	**2**	**3**
Duration	0–15secs	15secs–2mins	Over 2mins
Technical term	ATP–PC system	LA (lactic acid)	Aerobic system
Description	Strength, power, speed	Short-term muscular endurance	Long-term muscular endurance and aerobic activity
Rugby activities	Scrum-half burst	Prolonged 'rolling maul'	Prolonged open play, recovery between plays

ATP = adenosine triphosphate
PC = phosphocreatine

Fig 5   The main energy systems of the body and their practical meaning in Rugby.

cannot be sustained for long (*see* Fig 5). Anaerobic training will be considered later in this chapter.

Aerobic Endurance

Aerobic CR fitness is developed by progressively taxing the CR system (the heart, lungs, blood vessels and the blood itself) and so the most practical indication of aerobic training intensity is heart rate, or pulse. It is generally agreed that gains in CR fitness will occur when the heart rate (HR) is raised to a sufficient level for a 'training effect'. But what is a 'sufficient level'? As a general rule optimal gains in CR fitness occur when the HR is raised to within 60–90 per cent of maximum, where maximum is estimated as 220 minus your age (in years). This figure gives the number of beats per minute. For example:

Person: A. Robic
Age: 20 years
Estimated maximum HR:
220–20 = 200 beats per minute (bpm)
Training zone = 60–90% of max.
              = 120–180 bpm

This is likely to yield a conservative estimate at the lower end of the range for most active sportspeople, so another simpler, method is to add 25 to your age and subtract the sum from 220:

Person: A. Robic
Age: 20 years
CR training intensity
= 220–(20+25)
= 220–45
= 175 bpm

You can count your own pulse either at your wrist or your neck. At the wrist (the radial pulse) simply place three fingers (not your thumb) lightly on your upturned wrist at the base of the thumb. It is probably easier to count for fifteen seconds and then multiply by four for your bpm figure. Errors will occur but these should diminish with practice. A stronger pulse can be felt at the neck (the carotid pulse) by placing the fingers gently against the neck at the base of the angle of the jaw bone. For reasons of safety, you must not press too hard.

Fig 6 summarises the FITT principle for aerobic fitness training. This shows minimum criteria and many active sportspeople will require greater levels of training. Moreover, for maximum benefit in the game of Rugby

FITT component	Minimum criteria
Frequency	3 times per week
Intensity	Elevated heart rate 60–90% of maximum, or 220–(age + 25) beats per minute
Time	20 minutes
Type (of exercise)	Gross body exercise, such as running, swimming, cycling.

Fig 6   The FITT principle as applied to cardiorespiratory training.

the types of exercise used should be as relevant and similar to Rugby as possible. This suggests that swimming and cycling will not be as good for the Rugby player as running, and indeed running might best be done in 'interval' form to simulate the stop-start action of the game itself. However, it is important to remember that the CR system is central to recovery from all forms of exercise, so although some Rugby players (wingers, for example) need not have the running endurance of the long-distance athlete, they do need a fundamental base of adequate aerobic fitness.

A variety of aerobic-type running drills will be well-known to many players and coaches. Fig 7 shows how the pitch markings can be used to vary the distances of aerobic shuttle-running exercises. Longer distances for prolonged periods of time (routes 3 and 4) may be more applicable to forwards, while the backs need shorter runs (routes 1 and 2) but run at a faster pace. Both sets of exercises can be primarily aerobic if the activity is fairly continuous and the heart rate elevated throughout. Progressive overload can be achieved by requiring a faster time for the run, or by reducing the rest periods. Forwards can usually perform various body-weight exercises at the beginning and end of these shuttle-runs in order to simulate the action of running to a maul or ruck, performing muscular endurance work and then running on to the next phase of play.

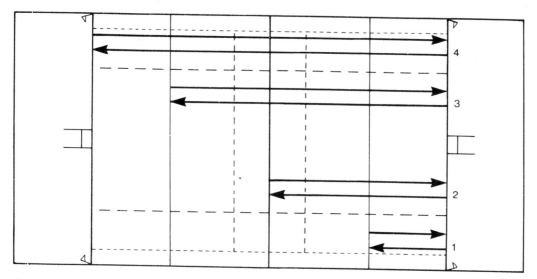

Fig 7   Aerobic training using the Rugby field.

At times, Rugby skills practices can be mixed in with these fitness routines. This can be useful for several reasons:

(i)   It provides a form of training similar to the actual game.
(ii)   Players can immediately see the point of the activity.
(iii) It allows for variety in fitness training.

However, caution needs to be exercised since the load placed on the player should not be so great that the skills are performed badly; fatigue is a major cause of skill breakdown – so beware.

Assessing Aerobic Fitness

The best way to use fitness tests is to compare scores over time for the same player so that progress can be tracked. Simple field tests can be used, such as recording the distance run around a track in twelve minutes, the time taken to run one and a half miles and so on. Assuming that the conditions (including the motivation of the player) stay the same from one test to the next, changes in scores give some indication of changing fitness levels. Another simple indication is to step up and down on a bench or stair approximately 50cm high (although the exact height does not greatly matter).

Perform for a set time, perhaps five minutes, to a definite rhythm or beat and then take your pulse. If this exercise is repeated at a later date in exactly the same way any change in the pulse gives some indication of CR fitness changes. Such simple methods can be appealing but are only rough guides to progress. With the growing availability of laboratory testing, more accurate measurement should be possible for a greater number of players.

The area of 'muscle fitness' will be considered next, but before proceeding, you should check the definitions of these terms in Fig 8. These different components of muscle fitness are often interrelated. For example, in order to develop power both strength and speed are necessary. For the sake of simplicity, however, most areas will be tackled separately, but you should bear in mind the overlap that does exist.

MUSCULAR ENDURANCE

This aspect of fitness follows on naturally from aerobic fitness. Since muscular endurance is the ability to *repeat* muscle contractions – such as repetition sit-ups – over time, improving this component of fitness requires a relatively high number of repetitions to be performed. This is the reverse of strength

Term	Definition
Strength	The maximum force that a muscle, or group of muscles, can generate. Sometimes the statement 'at a specified speed or velocity' can be added to this definition because force will diminish as the speed of the limb increases.
Muscular endurance	The ability of the muscle or muscle group to continue applying force.
Power	The product of force and velocity; in simpler terms strength × speed.
Flexibility	Range of motion about a joint or series of joints.

Fig 8   *Definition of terms applied to muscle fitness.*

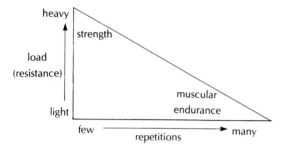

Fig 9   The strength-muscular endurance continuum.

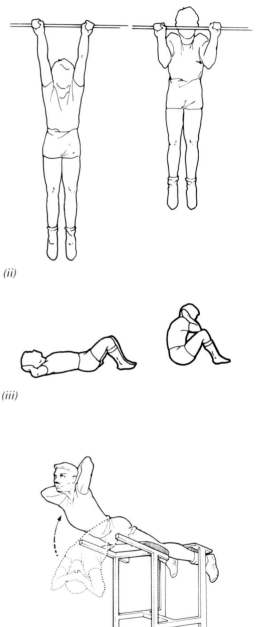

development, as explained later and illustrated in Fig 9. It is clearly the case that large numbers of repetitions can only be performed with a relatively small resistance. While this may be external resistance, such as weights, it is often sufficient simply to use body-weight, such as in press-ups and sit-ups. A series of basic body-weight endurance exercises is shown in Figs 10 and 11.

More specific application to Rugby can be made by constant repetition of certain game skills – for example, one-against-one mauling or repetition line-out jumping with ankle or wrist weights. However, care should be taken that the skills are replicated exactly. Other Rugby-specific exercises are shown in the section on strength development.

Fig 11   Muscular endurance exercises.
(i)   Press-ups.
(ii)   Pull-ups.
(iii)   Sit-ups.
(iv)   Back extensions.

Name	Figure	Muscle Action
Press-ups	11(i)	Back of upper arms (triceps) and chest
Pull-ups[2]	11(ii)	Front of upper arms (biceps), shoulders and upper back
Sit-ups[3]	11(iii)	Stomach
Back extensions[4]	11(iv)	Back muscles

Note: leg muscles may require additional resistance (see the leg exercises in the weight-training section of this chapter). People sometimes refer to 'pull-ups' (2) as involving an overgrasp grip and 'chins' an undergrasp grip. The effect is similar. You should always perform sit-ups (3) with bent legs, and for back extensions (4) you should not lift your shoulders far above your hips.

Fig 10   Basic body-weight muscular endurance exercises.

Assessing Muscular Endurance

Basic tests of muscular endurance are simple to perform, although always dependent on the subject performing at maximum effort and motivation. As with the CR tests, you can use them to plot individual progress. Any muscular endurance exercise can be used as a test as long as it can be easily measured – for example, the number of sit-ups performed in a set time. Of course, comparisons are only valid if the techniques are always the same.

STRENGTH AND POWER

No other area of physical fitness has suffered more than strength training from misunderstanding and mythology. The 'circus strongman' image still persists in many instances, yet it is just as easy to find slim 800m runners lifting weights as it is heavily-built shot-putters! Weight training, the most common of strength-training methods, is simply a way of increasing the resistance placed on the muscles to stimulate their growth and development. Whilst on this subject, some popular misconceptions need correction: women will not become masculine if they lift weights; it is not possible for muscle to turn into fat; weight training will not slow you down! Indeed modern-day

athletes use strength and power training extensively, although it must be said that some sports are more advanced in their methods than others. In short, there is no dynamic sport where some form of resistance training is not required.

Before proceeding, it is worth looking again at Fig 8. Very few sports involve maximum force at slow speeds and most require fast strength (power), although propping in Rugby is one of the few instances in which 'static' strength is required. However, because power is a combination of strength and speed, the two terms will be dealt with together and pure speed will be considered separately.

Without going into great detail on how muscles actually work, it is worth noting briefly that there are different types of muscle fibres. 'Slow-twitch' (ST or type I) fibres, as their name suggests, are endurance fibres with low power. The 'fast-twitch' (FT or type II) fibres are the opposite – powerful but only able to operate briefly. In fact, there are two subdivisions of these muscle fibres; type IIa and IIb fibres. The latter has a very fast-twitch action while type IIa fibres, although having a fast-twitch action also have some endurance capacity.

We all possess both ST and FT fibres in varying proportions, the ratio being determined by heredity. However, through a process of self-selection it is likely that

Characteristics	Slow twitch	Fast twitch
Aerobic capacity	High	Low
Anaerobic capacity	Low	High
Contraction time	Slow	Fast
Force	Low	High
Activities	Endurance-type	Sprint/explosive-type
Fatigue	Slow	Fast

Fig 12 Summary of characteristics of fast and slow-twitch muscle fibres, adapted from Fox, E.L., Sports Physiology *(Saunders College, 1979).*

marathon runners will have a high percentage of ST fibres and sprinters a high percentage of FT fibres, although there is probably great variation within these two extreme groups. Fig 12 summarises the differences between the two main types of fibres, and Fig 13 illustrates the order in which the fibres are always recruited.

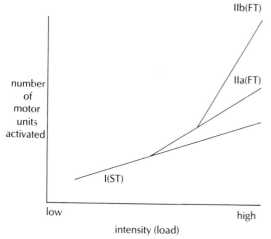

Fig 13 Recruitment pattern of muscle fibres.

This order (type I, type IIa, type IIb) and the associated intensity of exercise needed to bring about this recruitment show that heavy resistance and high intensity training (high loads with repetitions of six or less) is proba-

bly the best way to develop explosive strength. This contradicts the commonly held belief that heavy resistance training will slow you down. Once repetitions start to exceed about six, the initial tension on the muscle is reduced and less type IIb fibres recruited. This does not mean, of course, that pure speed training (as outlined later) is of no use – indeed it is very important for skill and neuro-muscular reasons and is likely to assist in the translation of power and strength development into a more functional form.

FT fibres can also be recruited through very fast actions – another form of increased intensity (*see* Fleck and Kraemer, 1987).

Types of Strength and Power Training Methods

There are several different ways of developing strength. A selection of these are as follows:

(i) Constant resistance (sometimes called isotonic); this is the conventional type of training involving barbells, dumbells and body-weight. Although called constant resistance, this is slightly inaccurate as the actual resistance on the muscle will change as the body levers create different forces (the weight on the bar, of course, does remain the same). This is probably the most accessible form of effective strength training for Rugby players.

(ii) Static resistance (isometric); force is

applied to an immovable object and so no movement is observed. This, however, is not a very useful form of training for some Rugby players because of its static nature, although some aspects of the game do require this form of strength training; binding together in the scrum, for example, is primarily a static form of strength, as is holding the scrum in a 'steady' position to allow for a controlled channelling of the ball to the scrum-half. (Static resistance training can be unsafe for older people as it creates sharp elevations in blood pressure.)

(iii) Same-speed training (isokinetic); performed with the aid of a machine which will only allow the limb to move at a set speed. The resistance on the muscle depends on the voluntary effort of the athlete. This form of training has some benefits for water sports and requires the use of special machines, such as isokinetic swim benches.

(iv) Variable resistance; performed on machines which vary the resistance put on the muscle through its range of movement. This helps overcome the inherent weakness of isotonic training in which the muscle is only working at maximal force in one part of the range of movement. However, variable resistance machines are still not readily available to all athletes and tend only to cater for single-joint actions. Since most sports demand actions which are multi-jointed a combination of isotonic and variable resistance exercise is desirable.

Exercises can, of course, be differentiated according to the part of the body you wish to develop such as lower, middle and upper. However, in addition to this it is worth splitting the exercises into three types, according to their function; general, specific and competition-specific.

General strength/power exercises are required by almost all sportspeople for basic increases in strength and power in the major muscle groups of the body, such as the legs, back and shoulders. Specific exercises are those which work the muscles particularly relevant to the sport in question, in this case Rugby, and competition-specific are those resistance exercises which copy, as closely as possible, the actual skills needed in the particular sport. For example, exercises for Rugby players might include scrummaging against a machine, or line-out jumping with ankle weights attached. Figs 14, 15 and 16 suggest some resistance exercises for each of these categories and are illustrated in Figs 17–32. Figs 33–35 explain how the exercises should be performed.

Figure	Exercise	Major muscles involved	Equipment
17	Power clean	Hips, legs, back (power development)	Barbell
18	Front squat	Hips, legs (quadriceps)	Barbell
19	Leg extension	Quadriceps	Machine
20	Leg curls	Hamstrings	Machine
21	Side bends	Oblique (side) abdominals	Dumbell
22	Bench press	Chest, triceps, shoulders	Barbell or machine
23	Arm curl	Biceps	Barbell or machine

Fig 14   *General resistance exercises for Rugby players.*

Figure	Exercise	Major muscles involved	Equipment
24	Split squats for hip flexibility)	Quadriceps (and	Barbell
25	Dumbell jump squats	Quadriceps, hips	Dumb-bell
26	Single-arm cheat rowing	Trunk rotators	Dumb-bells
27	Seated rowing	Side of chest ('lats'), upper back, biceps	Machine
28	Plyometric exercises	Hips, quadriceps, calves	Benches/gym boxes

Fig 15 Specific resistance exercises for Rugby players.

Figure	Exercise	Major muscles involved	Simulation of	Equipment
29	'Good mornings'	Back	Propping	Barbell
30	Neck exercises	Neck	Scrummaging	None
31	Resistance running	Quadriceps, hips,	Sprinting; breaking calves	Belt, rope tackles
32	Crouching dumbell	Triceps, shoulders, press	Line-out jumping quadriceps, hips	Dumbells

Fig 16 Competition-specific resistance exercises for Rugby players.

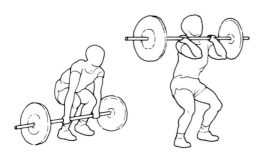

Fig 17 Power clean.

Fig 18 Front squat.

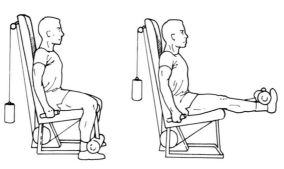

Fig 19 Leg extension.

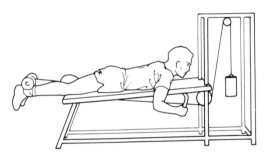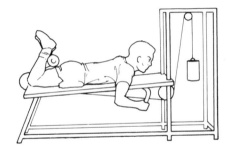

Fig 20   Leg curl.

Fig 21   Side bends.

Fig 22   Bench press.

Fig 24   Split squats.

Fig 23   Arm curls.

Fig 25 Dumb-bell jump squats.

Fig 26 Single-arm cheat rowing.

Fig 27 Seated rowing.

Fig 28 Plyometric exercises.

Fig 29 'Good mornings'.

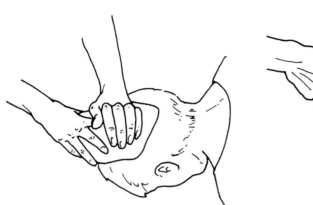
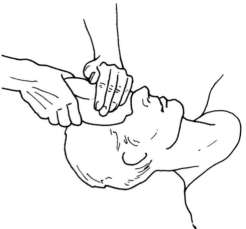

Fig 30   Neck exercises.

Fig 31   Resistance running.

Fig 32   Crouching dumb-bell press.

Figure	Exercise	Starting position	Movement	Other points
17	Power clean	Feet under bar, hip-width apart. Shoulder-width overgrasp grip. Hips below shoulders. Arms straight, back flat.	Lift bar from floor with straight arms and keep back flat. Extend body. Keep bar close in. Turn wrists over and receive bar on front shoulders. Bend legs to receive bar. Lower to thighs, then to floor.	Have bar 20 cm off the floor to begin. Use blocks or wooden disks for this. Make movement smooth and later fast and dynamic.
18	Front squat	Bar on chest, high elbows. Feet flat just outside hip-width.	Squat under control to 'thighs parallel'. Return to standing. Keep chest up throughout.	Avoid deep squatting.
19	Leg extension	Feet under lower pads. Sit upright.	Extend leg then lower under control.	
20	Leg curl	Face down on machine, heels under top pads.	Bring heels up towards buttocks. Return under control.	
21	Side bends	Stand with feet beyond hip-width. Dumbell in one hand at the side, other hand behind head or at the side.	Bend sideways with weight, return to middle position and beyond to position of stretch. Return to start.	Move sideways only. Do not use a dumbell in each hand.
22	Bench press	Lie face-up on a bench. Hips, shoulders, head all on bench. Shoulder-width grip of bar.	Lower bar to chest. Extend arms to straighten them fully.	If using a barbell rather than machine, beginners may find it easier to balance if they start to exercise with the bar on the chest.
23	Arm curl	Undergrasp grip on bar, upright body.	Pull bar to top of the chest, keeping elbows at the side of the body. Return under control.	

Note: although specific breathing techniques can be recommended for each exercise, it is often easier, particularly with beginners, simply to suggest that they breathe freely and naturally. Do *not* hold your breath during the execution of these exercises. This applies to all the exercises in Figs 17–32.

Fig 33   Explanation of general weight-training exercises.

Figure	Exercise	Starting position	Movement	Other points
24	Split squat	Bar on front shoulders, elbows high. Feet split front–back. Front foot flat, toes slightly pointed inwards. Rear foot on toes pointing forwards.	Bend front leg and push hips down and forward. Maintain upright trunk. Push back off front leg once thigh is parallel to floor.	Repeat exercise with other foot forwards.
25	Dumb-bell jump squats	Dumbell in each hand, stand with one foot in front of the other, legs bent.	Leap into the air, reverse foot position and land by bending the legs.	
26	Single-arm cheat rowing	Bend forward and support one arm on a bench. With the other arm, lift a dumbell. Feet split front and back.	Lift the dumbell and rotate the trunk so that the chest faces away from the bench.	
27	Seated rowing	Seated on the ground with legs straight. Face the upward pulley station. Overgrasp grip on bar.	Pull bar to chest, return under control.	Avoid swinging movements.
28	Plyometric exercises	These are bounding-type exercises with or without boxes for varying the height and depth of jumps.		

Fig 34   Explanation of specific weight-training exercises.

Figure	Exercise	Starting position	Movement	Other points
29	'Good mornings'	Bar resting on the shoulders behind the neck. Upright stance; feet beyond hip width.	Slowly lower shoulders by bending at the hips until shoulders are about 6–9" above waist height. Return to start position.	Keep knees slightly unlocked throughout. This is an advanced exercise to be attempted only by experienced weight trainers.
30	Neck exercises	A variety of resistance exercises for the neck can be attempted, see Fig 30.		
31	Resistance running		Normal sprint/run action	Ensure normal running action does not deteriorate with excessive resistance.
32	Crouching dumbell press	Start in the same position as for line-out jumping, dumbell in each hand at shoulder height.	Extend legs and arms. Return under control.	

Fig 35   Explanation of competition-specific resistance exercises.

	TIME		
	Preparation phase (out of season)	**Pre-competitive phase (pre-season)**	**Competitive phase (during season)**
Emphasis	Strength	Power	Power maintenance
Loading (intensity)	High	High	Medium
Exercises	Mainly general	General plus specific (some competition-specific)	Mainly specific and competition-specific
Frequency	2–3 times per week	2–3 times per week	2 times per week
Time (excluding warm-up and cool-down)	45–60mins	40mins	30mins

Fig 36   Developing strength and power across the training year.

Planning Strength and Power Training

You should always remember that strength and power training is merely an aid to improved performance in Rugby. The training should therefore be 'cycled' so that the maximum benefit is derived. This is a complex matter, but space permits only a brief discussion. Basically, strength/power training should develop across three phases of the year, starting at the end of the season. After a brief rest, the player should start a basic strength programme which should be largely made up from those exercises in Fig 14. As the season approaches, the training should become more dynamic and power-oriented. Exercises from Fig 15 can now be added and also, as the new season approaches, competition-specific exercises. During the season itself, the number of sessions may be reduced (perhaps from three to two per week), as now the aim is power maintenance. This process is shown in Fig 36. Using part of the FITT principle, the following guidelines can be offered to vary the training according to the individual.

(i) Beginner (with weight training)
Frequency: 2–3 times per week.
Intensity: low; all weights should be light enough to perform 8–10 repetitions in good style, 3 sets each exercise.
Time: initially short (30mins) but could increase to 45mins.

(ii) Intermediate
Frequency: 2–3 times per week.
Intensity: medium, occasionally high. Last few repetitions should be fairly hard (5 sets of 5 repetitions).
Time: up to 1 hour.

(iii) Advanced
Frequency: 3–4 times per week.
Intensity: varied, including occasional maximums.
Time: up to 1 hour.

The structure of each session should be (in the following order):
(i)   Warm-up.
(ii)   General exercises.
(iii)   Specific/competition-specific exercises.
(iv)   Cool-down.

Needs Assessment

In their excellent book *(Designing Resistance Training Programmes*, Human Kinetics 1987), giving advice on designing resistance training programmes, Fleck & Kraemer list a variety of important factors that should be assessed in planning a strength/power programme for an athlete. The three major 'needs assessment' categories identified are: exercise movements, metabolism used and injury prevention.

(i)   Exercise movements. The coach, in planning the strength/power programmes of the players, needs to know which specific muscles and muscle groups need to be developed. Questions which could be asked might include: are there any specific joint angles that need strengthening (perhaps the angle of the back in the scrum)? What should the emphasis be in terms of strength, power, endurance? Which type of exercise or exercises should be used (isotonic, isometric, isokinetic and so on)?

(ii)   Metabolism used. What is the estimated percentage contribution from each of the three main energy systems outlined in Fig 5?

(iii)   Injury prevention. Develop the most common sites of possible injury and select exercises *suitable* for sites of previous injuries.

Most of these factors require specialist weight-training coaches (such as those qualified through the BAWLA scheme) working in close co-operation with Rugby coaches.

Assessing Strength and.Power

Assessing strength and power is often recommended by coaches and fitness experts but the measurement of strength can be a problem, particularly for beginners who are unused to maximum muscular effort. This could be a dangerous form of exercise. Moreover, some exercises require the learning

of considerable skills before the athlete should attempt one repetition at maximum resistance. Although safer forms of strength testing, (such as grip-strength tests) do exist, they are of limited value in most sports contexts. What is more advantageous is to assess power and, in the case of Rugby, leg power.

Fortunately, measuring leg power is relatively easy although, as with all field tests of fitness, it gives only a rough indication of the fitness component. Two tests are well known; a standing long jump and a standing vertical jump (*see* Fig 37). These can be used to gauge the likely effectiveness of certain players in, for example, the line-out. The jump tests can also be used to assess progress in the resistance training programme – improvements in leg power should occur after such a programme.

Additional Considerations in Strength and Power Training

Safety

Weight-training has an excellent safety record – particularly so when weight-trainers

Fig 37   Vertical-jump test.

lift in a well-planned environment with good supervision. Nevertheless, like most activities, a safety code should be adhered to. The following are the main points to note.

Personal safety:
(i)   Learn correct techniques.
(ii)   Train with other people so they can help out if necessary.
(iii) Warm up properly.
(iv)   Wear appropriate clothing, including training shoes.
(v)   Progress gradually through a planned schedule.

External Safety:
(i)   Check all apparatus before use.
(ii)   Keep all apparatus well maintained and hygienic.
(iii) Ensure the floor space is free of obstacles, such as loose disks.
(iv)   Plan the floor space for maximum, but safe, use.
(v)   Determine the maximum number of people who can use the facility safely and do not exceed this number.

Children's safety:
When encouraging youngsters into sport it is always tempting to give them the same training programme as adults, but this is a mistake, especially with strength/power exercises. It is generally recommended that pre-pubertal children should not lift heavy weights, although light exercises are unlikely to cause harm. Depending upon the child's development, thirteen or fourteen years is probably the right age at which to start a weight-training programme in which the emphasis should be on technique and skill learning under qualified supervision.

SPEED TRAINING

Rugby players who have conscientiously trained with resistance exercises, especially the power exercises such as the power clean (Fig 17) or plyometrics (Fig 28) should find that their overall movement speed has improved. There are, however, different types of speed in sport. The ability to react quickly to a stimulus is called reaction time and in Rugby is best illustrated by the reaction of the hooker to the ball being fed into the scrum – reaction time here is the time between the stimulus, the signal that the ball is coming into the scrum, and the start of the movement. Reaction time can be improved with practice, but only so far; hookers will never be able to react at exactly the same moment as the ball is put into the scrum.

Equally important in sport is the ability to react *and move* (response time). It is little help to react quickly (mentally) when the ball is being fed into the scrum if you are a slow striker of the ball! It is also important, in sprinting speed for example, to be able to maintain your speed (speed endurance). Sometimes, however, it is better to have controlled speed rather than flat-out speed which may create some technical problems. For example, it may be better to run just less than flat out but then draw the opposition and give a well-timed pass rather than simply to run at full speed and not have the control needed to give a good pass.

Given the strength and power training already outlined, the Rugby player is advised to combine this with speed and agility drills. Here are some examples:

(i)   Shuttle running across small sectors of the pitch.
(ii)   Pressure drills requiring good response time (for example, catching and giving passes at speed)
(iii) Sprint drills.

Often response speed can be improved simply through experience because the player has become more efficient at reading the game and so is more likely to be able to anticipate what will happen next.

Assessing Speed and Agility

Assessing sprint speed is relatively easy, although the validity of such measures will depend upon the accuracy of the timekeeper. Also, the distance used for sprint time-trials should be matched to the requirements of the players. A 40m sprint is often used as a measure of the type of speed needed in field team games such as Rugby.

Agility is a desirable characteristic in Rugby, particularly for backs. An excellent means of testing agility is the Illinois agility run, shown in Fig 38. However, since this involves running for over fifteen seconds, a shorter and more dynamic test might be even more appropriate for Rugby. An example of such a test is given in Fig 39 – the Nebraska Agility Test, originally designed for American footballers but which also provides a useful test for Rugby players. Of course, there is no reason why Rugby coaches should not devise their own agility test along similar lines.

FLEXIBILITY TRAINING

Flexibility is the most neglected area of sports fitness! Certainly this is the case for most sports (with the possible exceptions of gymnastics, swimming and some athletics events). Most games players are notoriously inflexible! However, flexibility is important for several reasons:

(i)   Enhanced flexibility can help in the prevention and rehabilitation of injury.
(ii)   Poor flexibility can inhibit the development of some sports skills.
(iii)   Poor flexibility can reduce the effectiveness of other fitness parameters.

In essence, flexibility is not just for dancers and gymnasts. Serious Rugby players also need good flexibility (which really means the range of movement at a joint or joint complex) and should be spending five or ten minutes a day stretching.

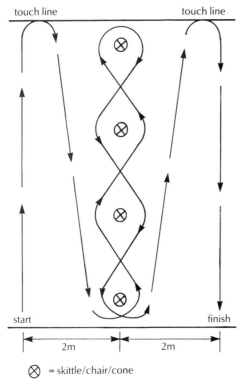

⊗ = skittle/chair/cone

Note: start position is lying face down on floor with hands by the shoulders and head on the start line.

Fig 38   Illinois agility run, reproduced with permission from Adams, J. et al., Foundations of Physical Activity *(Stipes, 1965).*

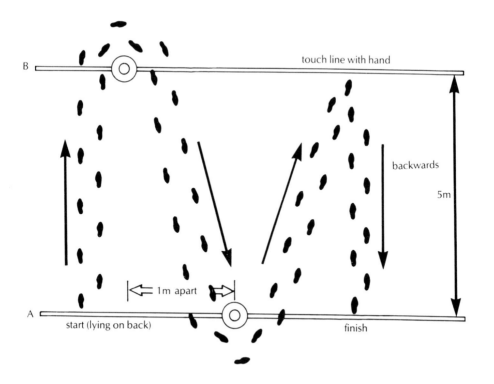

B — touch line with hand

backwards

5m

1m apart

A — start (lying on back) — finish

Fig 39   Nebraska agility test, reproduced with permission from Epley,
B., The Strength of Nebraska (University of Nebraska, 1980).

Methods of Flexibility Training

There are three main forms of flexibility training: static flexibility; ballistic flexibility and PNF (proprioceptive neuromuscular facilitation!).

Static Flexibility

This method involves stretching a muscle to the point of *mild tension* and then holding it statically for a length of time in the stretched position. This time may vary but it should not be for less than ten seconds. Although some people suggest at least thirty seconds, this can be boring and may lead to players neglecting their flexibility training.

Static stretching is a very effective means of improving flexibility and is recommended for all Rugby players. It should always be performed prior to vigorous activity and before ballistic flexibility exercises. The best time to improve flexibility is when the muscles are warm, so after a game or training is often

		stop here
Preparatory Stretch	Developmental Stretch	Forceful Over-stretch
as part of warm-up	to improve flexibility	too much
to prepare for activity	best done after vigorous exercise	don't

Fig 40   The stretch continuum.

67

ideal. However, static stretching should also be performed as part of the warm-up as mentioned at the beginning of this chapter. (Fig 40 shows the stretch continuum.) Players should not overstretch in the belief that more must be better. You should stretch to the point of mild tension, not pain!

Partners can be used to help stretch a little further, but remember that the athlete stretching must be in charge. This is particularly important to stress when groups of children are performing flexibility exercises.

Ballistic Flexibility

A further type of flexibility is ballistic stretching. Here the muscles are stretched by using bouncing or bobbing movements at the end of the range. There has been some controversy over this type of stretching since it has been implicated as a cause of injury. However, while it should never be recommended for people on health-related exercise programmes (particularly older people or those with a history of joint injury), it is beneficial for sportspeople as most sports require participants to stretch while moving. The obvious example is the hurdler who performs ten ballistic stretches in each race. Ballistic stretching, therefore, *is* a necessary part of sport, but precautions must be taken to avoid injury. Such precautions should include a good warm-up (including static stretches) to prepare the body for more ballistic activity. Care should be taken that at the end of the range of motion the bouncing or bobbing is both controlled and gradual. These types of stretches should be specific to the movement required in Rugby.

PNF Flexibility

PNF is a more advanced and highly effective method of stretching. It involves three basic stages:

(i)   Contraction of the muscle to be stretched (for about ten seconds).
(ii) Relaxation of the same muscle.
(iii) Contraction of the antagonist (opposite) muscle or the use of partner assistance to stretch the muscle.

The technique is believed to be effective because the initial muscular contraction allows the muscle to be stretched further. Most of the exercises shown can be adapted for PNF, but you should remember that the muscular contraction will not be effective without something to work against and so apparatus or partner resistance is required. You should use the static method when stretching during PNF (*see* Figs 41 and 42 for explanations of the flexibility exercises and also Figs 43–53).

Problem Flexibility Exercises

Not all flexibility exercises are necessarily good exercises. Because the muscles are being stretched, a strain is being put on the joints. In most cases, the joints (as well as ligaments and tendons) are being stretched in an acceptable way, but sometimes the joint can be twisted or put under pressure in such a way that the exercise is potentially harmful. Figs 54 and 55 show two of the most common flexibility exercises which should, as a general rule, be avoided.

The ballistic standing toe touch can lead to back problems and should *never* be performed by anyone who has experienced back trouble in the past. It is better for all athletes to use the sit and reach exercise in Fig 57. The hurdler stretch (Fig 55) may lead to problems for those with knee injuries and although this exercise can be effective in improving the flexibility of the hamstrings and groin, it puts a great deal of pressure on the knee joint. However, given the likelihood of knee injuries in Rugby, this exercise is best avoided.

Figure	Exercise	Muscle stretched	Starting position	Movement	Other points
43	Calf	Calf	Lean against wall, foot pointing forwards.	(i) To stretch outer calf, keep leg straight and push heel into ground. Push hips forwards. (ii) To stretch inner calf (soleus), bend leg and push forwards and downwards with hip. Keep heel on ground.	Vary position of toes.
44	Hamstring and lower back stretch	Hamstrings, lower back	Sit on floor, feet together and legs straight.	Sit up first (chest out) then stretch forwards to the toes.	Vary leg positions (apart).
45	Hip stretch	Front of hip	Lunge position on floor.	Push hips forwards.	Progress to more upright trunk position with rear foot on toes.
46	Groin stretch	Groin, inside of thighs	Sit on floor, legs folded with soles of feet together.	Gently ease knees outwards and downwards.	Use pressure from arms if necessary.
47	Side stretch	Side (oblique) abdominals	Upright stance, feet astride.	Bend sideways and hold position.	Avoid leaning forwards.
48	Shoulder stretch	Shoulders, chest	(i) Standing. (ii) Seated – leg in front.	Lift arms upwards and backwards. Partner lifts arms upwards and backward, or sideways.	(iii) If partner places a knee in the back of the exerciser, this can help stability.
49	Wrist stretch	Forearms	Kneeling on floor, hands flat.	Fingers pointing towards the body, pull shoulders back to stretch forearms.	Change direction of fingers.
50	Arm stretch	Shoulder, side of chest	Kneeling on all fours arm outstretched.	Pull shoulder back to produce stretch on top of shoulder, arm and side of chest.	Reach out with hand first.
51	Lying stretch	(all-round stretch)	Lying face-up on floor.	Extend body position as much as possible.	

Fig 41 Explanations of static flexibility exercises.

Figure	Exercise	Muscles stretched	Starting position	Movement	Other points
52	PNF Hamstring stretch	Hamstrings	Sitting on floor, feet together and legs straight.	Contraction: push back against partner and push down into the ground with both legs (10secs), then relax. Stretch: reach forwards (with or without partner assistance) towards toes.	
53	PNF shoulder stretch	Shoulder, chest	Sitting or kneeling, arms outstretched to the side, parallel with floor.	Contraction: pull arms forwards against partner resistance (10secs), then relax. Stretch: partner pulls arms back, keeping them parallel to the floor.	Can also be done with arms above head.

Fig 42   Explanations of PNF flexibility exercises.

Fig 43   Calf stretch.

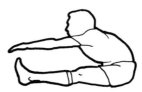

Fig 44   Hamstring and lower back stretch.

Fig 45   Hip stretch.

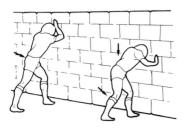

Fig 46   Groin stretch.

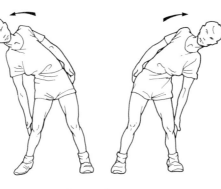

Fig 47   Side stretch.

Fig 48   Shoulder stretch.

Fig 49   Wrist stretch.

Fig 50   Arm stretch.

Fig 51   Lying stretch.

Fig 52   PNF hamstring stretch.

Fig 53   PNF shoulder stretch.

Fig 54   Ballistic standing toe touch.

Fig 55   Hurdler stretch.

FITT component	Suggested guidelines
Frequency	Can be done every day once some experience has been gained. Initially, every other day.
Intensity	To point of mild tension in the stretched muscle.
Time	Each exercise 10–30secs. Each session 5–15mins.
Type (of exercise)	Static stretches, followed by PNF and ballistic. Progress from preparatory to developmental stretching.

Fig 56   FITT principle for flexibility exercises.

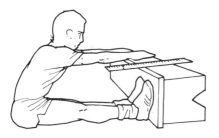

Fig 57   Sit and reach flexibility test.

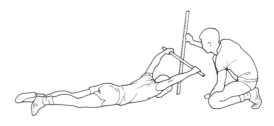

Fig 58   Lying shoulder reach test.

Fig 59   Behind back shoulder flexibility test.

Developing flexibility, like the other components of fitness, requires planning. Fig 56 summarises the FITT principle as it relates to flexibility training for Rugby players.

Assessing Flexibility

Any of the flexibility exercises may be used as tests by simply recording measurements. However, two tests of flexibility are particularly recommended. The first is the sit and reach test and provides a good indication of flexibility in the hamstrings and lower back – an important part of the body in which to have good flexibility since it can help prevent lower back problems. This test is shown in Fig 57.

The second flexibility test is the lying shoulder reach test (Fig 58); it is particularly important to have good shoulder flexibility in some positions (second-row, for example). Another way to see whether your shoulder

flexibility is symmetrical is to try the test in Fig 59. You will probably be better with one hand uppermost than with the other, showing that shoulder flexibility is usually uneven; flexibility exercises are useful in remedying this.

CHAPTER COOL-DOWN!

After covering the main aspects of physical fitness for Rugby, it is appropriate to cool down before moving on to the next chapter! This cool-down is a summary of the main points:

(i)   Physical fitness is multidimensional. The main components requiring physical training are: cardiorespiratory fitness (stamina), muscular endurance, strength, power, speed and flexibility.
(ii)   Proper planning of fitness training must take into account the frequency, intensity, time and type of exercises (FITT principle), as well as specificity and reversibility.
(iii)   Rugby players should always warm up and cool down before and after training or a match.
(iv)   Some Rugby players (particularly forwards) require high levels of aerobic fitness but should also be well trained in strength, power, speed and muscular endurance.
(v)   Some Rugby players (particularly backs) also require aerobic fitness but should concentrate more on power/speed training.
(vi)   Flexibility is a neglected aspect of fitness and is an important fitness component in Rugby.

3   Healthy Eating

Players must be well prepared physically on the day of competition. This preparation, of course, involves many training sessions over the previous months or years. Over this time, food has provided the energy for the players to maintain the body and to train. Nutrients in the food – protein, vitamins and minerals – have been used to replenish body losses incurred on a day to day basis. Food is, of course, crucial for the training process.

Food can also be important on psychological and social levels. It may be psychologically important to eat favourite foods or those believed to help performance. For this reason (and probably this reason alone) these foods (often highly peculiar to an individual) are eaten to ensure peak performance is reached and maintained. We all enjoy eating socially with a group of friends and do not want to appear too odd by choosing particularly unusual foods. Accordingly players may even choose foods which they know are unsuitable. If this happens on an occasional basis it does not matter, but if it is a regular occurrence then it is important to ask why this is the case. It must be emphasised that performance on the day depends primarily on the long period of preceding training (which includes diet).

Eating for your sport can be broken down into two subdivisions; eating for training (which also means for good health), and eating for matches. Both are influenced by who we are, where we are and the company we keep.

REQUIREMENTS FOR FOOD

Eating and drinking is taken for granted by most people. We eat and drink without too much thought and assume that our bodily needs will be met and indeed most of the time they are. However, whether these needs are being met optimally is the question that all serious sportspeople and their coaches should address.

The human body is marvellously resilient, tolerant and versatile. If food-energy intake is less than the body needs the body conserves energy in order to 'balance the books'. People on reducing diets have been observed to be less active and physically slower (thereby conserving energy) than before embarking on their diet. This has implications for the athlete who is training and deliberately reducing food intake. Is the same effort being put into the training or, indeed, can it be? When fed less than they need, young children become less active and grow less quickly as the body attempts to balance its 'energy books'. If a young player is exercising hard, but not able to eat a sufficient amount, it is likely that growth and/or the rate of exercise will suffer. It is not possible to get energy out if insufficient is consumed.

However, there comes a point when the body can no longer adapt to an insufficient intake of food-energy and at this point functions begin to deteriorate very noticeably. Body tissues are not repaired efficiently (they may be broken down and not replaced at all), levels of activity become poor and general health often deteriorates with increased likelihood of infection. Professional medical investigation and treatment may be essential at this point.

The body thus has an adaptive capability and a deficiency response. At the other end of the spectrum (and much more likely to occur in Western countries) the body reacts to excessive food-energy intake. Food consumption above requirement will not raise the level of activity or turn individuals into super-performers, although it will encourage rapid growth – in children upwards, and in adults outwards! Eating more protein than the body needs or can use simply results in the excess being excreted. The same is true of water-soluble vitamins such as vitamin C and some minerals such as sodium chloride (salt). In the case of fat-soluble vitamins such as vitamin A, and certain minerals such as iron which the body cannot so easily dispose of, excess stores can ultimately be life-threatening. Players, therefore, need to take special care with regard to the dangers of over-indulgence, especially when it comes to diet supplements. Regular monitoring of body-weight can provide information about meeting nutrient requirements or meeting them in excess!

Indeed there is a publication entitled *Recommended Amounts of Food Energy and Nutrients for Groups of People in the UK* (DHSS, 1979) which provides a useful guide. There is no evidence that sportspeople need any more food than non-sportspeople, providing that they are eating a good variety of foods which will meet their energy needs. These needs may well vary from season to season and during different training periods. The total amount of food consumed may therefore also vary.

In summary, the overall needs of the player in training will be both variable and to that athlete unique. This variation may be masked by the ability of the individual to adapt to different levels of nutrition, but it is essential that such adaptation is not allowed to mask impending deficiency. Players and their coaches must remain vigilant.

WHAT'S IN FOOD?

Food is a mixture of nutrients: fat, carbohydrate, protein, vitamins and minerals. Everyone needs these nutrients in the same way. Eating food ultimately enables these nutrients to be made available to our bodies. All naturally occurring foods contain all nutrients, but in differing amounts (dependent upon the function which the food performed in the plant or animal). For example, leaves are not storage organs and so their energy content is low. Meat, however, is largely muscle and so has a high protein content.

In Fig 60 there is a list of foods and some of the nutrients they contain. A more comprehensive list is given in the *Manual of Nutrition* (HMSO, 1985).

Sources of Carbohydrate

(Milk and milk products also provide significant amounts of calcium).

1 glass of milk	Supplies about 8g protein, 12g CHO, 8g fat, 150kcals.

For reduced energy and fat:

1 glass skimmed milk or 1 carton plain yoghurt	Supplies about 8g protein, 12g CHO, 80kcals.

Cereals and legumes – high carbohydrate and some protein.
1 thin/medium slice white bread*
½ roll, bun, crumpet, teacake etc.
1 tbs white flour*
1 digestive biscuit
   (also contains one portion of fat)
4 tbs unsweetened breakfast cereal*
3 tbs baked beans* or other cooked
   bean*/pea*/lentil*
   (also contains one third of portion
   of 'meat' protein)
3–4 tbs fresh/processed peas
1 tbs apple crumble/pie
   (also contains one portion of fat
   and one 'fruit' carbohydrate
   portion)

Each portion supplies about 2g protein, 15g CHO as starch and 70 kcals.

Fruit and vegetables – also supply important vitamins.
Small apple, pear, orange
½ small banana
10–12 cherries or grapes
2 medium plums, prunes, apricots,
   dates (dried)
1 tbs raisins, currants
2 tbs any vegetable (except avocado –
   add four portions of fat)
1 small/medium potato, boiled or
   baked (if fried add one portion of fat)

Each portion supplies about 0–2g protein, 5–10g CHO as sugars and 25–40kcals.

Sources of Fat

Small scrap butter or margarine (5g)
1 tsp oil
2 tsp mayonnaise
1 slice fried streaky bacon
5 olives
10 roasted peanuts
2 tsp double cream

Each portion supplies about 5g fat, 45kcals.

Sources of Protein

Meat and fish – also rich sources of minerals.

60–85g cooked (not fried) meat* or
   oily fish
60g hard cheese
85g edam, gouda, brie or similar
   cheese

Each portion supplies about 20–25g protein, 15–20g fat, 200–250kcals.

3 grilled sausages (add one portion of fat)
For reduced energy and fat:
60–85g cooked chicken (no skin), veal
   or rabbit
60–85g cooked liver*
60–85g white fish
60–85g tuna in brine or 4 pilchards
170g cottage cheese

Each portion supplies about 20–25g protein, 5g fat, 150kcals, but do not fry or add fat

Fig 60a   Nutrients contained in typical portions of food.

Sources of Thiamin or Vitamin B1

Milk and milk products	all milk and soya milk
Cereals and legumes	all legumes**, fortified (non-wholemeal) bread**, flour products and fortified breakfast cereals
Meat and fish	ham and pork products, liver
Fruit and vegetables	none
Other	brewers' yeast

Sources of Riboflavin or Vitamin B2

Milk and milk products	all types of milk**
Cereals and legumes	only fortified breakfast cereals
Meat and fish	liver
Fruit and vegetables	dark-green leafed vegetables
Other	brewers' yeast

Sources of Pyridoxine or Vitamin B6

Milk and milk products	none
Cereals and legumes	all legumes**
Meat and fish	beef, pork, lamb, tuna and salmon
Fruit and vegetables	bananas and potatoes
Other	nuts

Sources of Calcium

Milk and milk products	all milk**, cheese**, yoghurt

Cereals and legumes	fortified flour products, tofu
Meat and fish	salmon and sardines if bones consumed
Fruit and vegetables	dark-green leafed vegetables
Other	molasses and unhulled sesame seeds (as in tahini)

Sources of Iron

Milk and milk products	none
Cereals and legumes	fortified flour and products**, fortified breakfast cereals, all legumes**
Meat and fish	red meats**, liver**
Fruit and vegetables	dark-green leafed vegetables
Other	molasses, chocolate and cocoa

Sources of Zinc

Milk and milk products	cheese
Cereals and legumes	all legumes, bread, wholemeal flour and products
Meat and fish	meat**, liver, crab and shellfish
Fruit and vegetables	very small amounts in most fruit and vegetables
Other	nuts

* also rich in iron
** particularly rich source

Fig 60b   Sources of vitamins and minerals.

THE NEED FOR FLUID, ENERGY AND NUTRIENTS

Fluid

Our bodies are about seventy per cent water, so in a 70kg person 49kg is water. Cells (the constituents of every living thing) and blood need water in order to dissolve and to carry nutrients. Even a slight reduction in body water of two to five per cent (1.5–3.5l, 3–6pts) can cause a reduced efficiency in cellular function. Dehydration also does not allow the body sufficient water to cool itself and so the body may overheat. This makes us feel disorientated and undoubtedly reduces performance. Fluid balance or hydration must therefore be of prime importance to all sportspeople, including Rugby players. Water is normally lost in three ways:

(i)   Through urine. This volume is increased by taking more water or by certain nutrients such as alcohol (which has a diuretic effect).

(ii)   Through the skin (sweat). This normally accounts for a small percentage, but during exercise can rise to over 3l per hour, depending on the intensity of exercise and the environmental conditions.
(iii)   Through the lungs.

Water can also be lost *abnormally* in two ways:
(i)   Through diarrhoea. This may be caused by infection or by eating too much fibre or simple carbohydrate, which cannot be absorbed; this also causes water to be drawn into the gut from the body tissues (causing cell dehydration).
(ii)   Through fevers; water is lost via the skin to reduce body temperature.

Clearly, it is important to avoid extra fluid loss and this means taking care not to consume foods of dubious origin (including ice cubes) and choosing carbohydrate foods wisely. (*See* later in this chapter.)

Replacing the fluid lost during training and matches is also vital. Our normal thirst 'mechanisms' do not operate successfully at this level of loss and so are unreliable. Water loss therefore needs to be monitored actively, which means weighing before and after any exercise. The change in weight will reflect the loss of body water – which must be replaced. The best way to do this is to use a drink which is 'isotonic' to body fluids (the same concentration) or 'hypotonic' (weaker concentration): the drink should *never* be 'hypertonic' (more concentrated) as body fluid is drawn into the gut to dilute it (*see* above). This causes (osmotic) diarrhoea and is counter-productive.

It has been found that a solution of: 2.5g of sugar per 100 ml (about 1/2oz per pint), 23 mg of sodium (1.0 mmol) per 100 ml (a very small pinch per pint), 20 mg (0.5 mmol) of potassium per 100 ml (a smaller pinch per pint), served cold (as from the fridge) in about half pint quantities is ideal. Fortunately a dilute solution of orange squash (two to three tablespoons per pint) is just about the correct concentration. If using a commercially prepared drink, it is wise to check the concentration, which should not be greater than those given above. Plain water is also acceptable. Whatever is chosen, it is important to consume a replacement amount. One litre weighs about 1kg (2lb) and is equivalent to about two pints. It takes some practice and training to consume the quantities required. A drink containing alcohol causes extra urinary loss of water (it is a diuretic) and so should be avoided, so . . .

Pints of Beer Will Not Do!

Finally, individuals can prepare beforehand for the fluid which will be lost during a match. By carefully monitoring losses during training and matches it is possible to make predictions and consume sufficient fluid in advance to replace anticipated losses. Fluid intake at half-time may be necessary and could even affect the final result. It should not be necessary to take any extra food-energy at half-time unless it is to satisfy psychological demands – the energy stored in the body should be more than sufficient.

However, it is possible to enrich a drink with sugar and so provide additional carbohydrate although it will take about thirty minutes to be absorbed and appear in the bloodstream. This sugary solution will also reduce the rate at which fluid is absorbed, so individuals will have to decide which is the greater need – fluid or energy. The relative merits of fluid and energy replacement during a match are discussed further in the section on competition.

Requirements for Energy and Nutrients

The nutritional requirements of each player will depend on several factors, including age, sex and body-weight (growing children or teenagers need proportionally greater amounts of food than adults, while women need more iron than men and men need more energy because they often weigh more) and duration and intensity of exercise.

The above list is particularly applicable when considering the amount of energy required. It is less applicable with regard to the need for protein, minerals and vitamins.

ENERGY

Energy is derived from fat and carbohydrate (CHO) in food and, to a lesser extent, protein. The amount of energy in food is measured in units corresponding to the amount of heat that food would produce when it is 'burned' in the body. The heat produced can be thought of as providing the power to make the body work in much the same way as a coal fire produces heat to make steam to turn an engine. These units of 'heat' are calories.

A calorie is a very tiny amount of heat and the amount in food is thousands of calories or kilocalories (kcals). Another unit which is used to measure the amount of energy in food is the joule – again a very tiny unit of 'work-energy' and so expressed in kilojoules (kJ). One kilocalorie is equivalent to 4.2 kilojoules (1 kcal = 4.2 kJ). Large amounts of kilojoules are expressed as megajoules (MJ) – there are 1,000 kJ to a megajoule.

Energy in the food is used to do 'internal work'; it keeps the heart beating and the lungs and other organs working, even when we are asleep. This basic, essential requirement for energy is known as the basal metabolic rate (BMR) and varies with body size. BMR has the first priority for energy, however much is ingested. The other basic needs for energy are the renewal of body tissues and the excretion of waste products. After these energy requirements have been met, dietary energy is used for 'external' work. The amount of external work performed can be moderated to fit the dietary energy supply. The energy devoted to the synthesis of new tissue can also be moderated as the extra energy required for the synthesis of 1 kg (2 lb) of new tissue has been estimated to be as high as 5000 to 7000 kcals (about 21 to 29.4 MJ) above normal dietary intake.

SOURCES OF ENERGY

Carbohydrates as Dietary Sources of Energy

Plants store their energy as carbohydrate (CHO). This is a term used to cover a variety of molecules which all have similar chemical properties. Some molecules are small, taste sweet and are known as simple, or sugary, carbohydrate. They include glucose, sucrose (sugar), fructose, maltose and lactose (although lactose is an anomaly since animals produce it in milk for their young). Some molecules are large, do not taste sweet and are called complex, or starchy, carbohydrate (the starches in bread, potatoes, rice and pasta are all complex). Finally, there are some forms of carbohydrate which we cannot digest or absorb and are known as unavailable carbohydrate or dietary fibre. Eventually *all* dietary sources of the sugary and starchy carbohydrate, sometimes collectively called available CHO, will be transformed into glucose in the blood.

Each gram of available CHO provides 4kcals of energy to the body. It is found in all foods of plant origin: cereals, fruit, vegetables (including pulses such as dried peas, beans and lentils) and to a limited extent in nuts (*see* Fig 60). Fruit and vegetables contain a very high percentage of water and the carbohydrate which is present is much diluted. For this reason these foods are less 'energy-dense', which also applies to other nutrients which are similarly 'diluted'. It also means that to consume a large amount of energy a great quantity of these foods needs to be eaten. This is useful for slimmers, but not necessarily for the person who requires a high energy intake in a hurry. However, foods made from cereal grains (bread, pasta and biscuits or cakes and so on) do not contain as much water and so are more energy-dense. Bread, breakfast cereals, pasta and rice are all rich sources of CHO and are relatively energy-dense.

Once the CHO is consumed it appears in the blood as glucose. This can then be used directly for energy or stored in the muscle or in the liver as glycogen, the 'animal equivalent' of starch – a very important source of energy to all animal cells. There is a finite amount of glycogen which can be stored, about 200g (7oz). The glycogen stored in the muscle probably determines the amount of work which can be done by that muscle, while any excess glucose is then made into fat and stored in the adipose tissue.

Fats as Dietary Sources of Energy

Fat is found in almost all foods, since it is an important part of the cell wall of all plant and animal tissue. Plants do not store energy as fat (except in nuts) so the amount of fat in plant sources of food will be very low. Animals, including humans, store energy in their bodies as fat; indeed an average man may have 14kg (30lbs) of fat in his body. This fat is stored in many places; in adipose tissue around vital organs, under the skin and amongst muscle fibres. Therefore meat or animal products such as eggs, milk and milk products all contain fat, often in significant amounts (*see* Fig 60).

Fat is energy-dense and supplies 9kcals per gram, more than twice as much per unit weight as CHO. Animal products do not contain as much water as fruit and vegetables and so are doubly more energy- and nutrient-dense. Fat can also taste nice; think of the taste of fried mushrooms compared to boiled or the taste of buttered rather than dry toast! Eating fat is easy and because it is energy-dense it provides energy in small amounts of food; hence over-indulgence is easy, too. Active and busy athletes need this form of energy which can be eaten in a hurry, but the slimmer needs to beware!

Sources of Energy in the Diet and Long-Term Health

The amount and type of food-energy we consume may influence our health. It is generally agreed that there is a weight–height ratio at which adults are fitter and less prone to develop various life-threatening diseases. The more fat you carry, the higher will be the ratio and the more likely are such diseases. A simple way to calculate whether your weight–height ratio is satisfactory is to use this internationally-accepted method: weight (kg) divided by height (metres) squared. This is termed the body mass index (or BMI). The range thought to be acceptable is 17–25. If it is below the bottom end this is just as disturbing as if it is too high. If weight is reduced too far, this indicates poor body reserves of nutrients because of a restrictive dietary intake. A very restrictive intake can lead to nutrient deficiencies which will ultimately affect performance.

This weight–height ratio (BMI) is a simple and quick test. However, it does not tell us how much of an individual is fat, and how much is lean (muscle) tissue. To find out the ratio of fat to lean tissue a more specific measurement has to be made. One method which can be used is based on the assumption that the fat under the skin is a fair reflection of total body fat. Using special, skinfold callipers (*see* Fig 61) the amount of fat under the skin can be assessed. The total body fat can then be estimated by using a formula (Eisenman and Johnson, 1982). (Women, for physiological reasons, have a higher percentage of body fat than men.) The amount of fat which different people have varies and can be manipulated by the use of exercise and diet, although the difference between men and women always remains. A list of measured body fats is given below:

Average adult man (20–50 years)
    15–25 per cent fat
Average adult female (20–50 years)
    26–35 per cent fat
Adult male (distance) runner
    6–13 per cent fat
Adult female (distance) runner
    15–19 per cent fat

Adult male Rugby player
    about 19 per cent fat

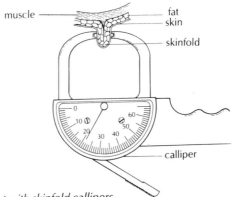

Fig 61 Estimating body fat with skinfold callipers.

The type of 'energy' consumed may have an effect on long-term health. It is thought advisable to consume the majority of energy in the form of carbohydrate. Sugary carbohydrates can cause dental disease and therefore reliance should be on the complex, or starchy, carbohydrates. Fats are thought to be associated with heart disease and certain forms of cancer and for these reasons are best avoided in large amounts. The saturated fats found in animal sources are thought to be more harmful than the fats from vegetable sources which are largely unsaturated.

The development of certain diseases which mainly afflict people in the developed countries is probably due to a number of factors, but two of them are diet and lack of exercise. At this time it is difficult to say how 'protective' exercise, practised intensively, will be in the long term. Certainly, it is important for Rugby players to meet energy and food needs, which may mean eating more fat than would normally be advised for the general public. But what the effects on long-term health are we simply do not know.

PROTEIN

The requirement for dietary protein depends on several factors, including: the amount of muscle tissue present (the more muscle tissue, the more body protein there is to maintain and replace); the amount of new tissue synthesis (in the growth phase proportionally more protein is required and also there is increased demand for energy for synthesis); the amount lost through sweat and hair/skin loss.

Much controversy surrounds the nature and extent of the body's needs for protein. The body can become very efficient at conserving its store of protein which is found in every cell in the body. It would seem that sportspeople need the same amount of protein per kilogram of body-weight as untrained individuals, although they will need more if energy supplies are not sufficient to meet demand, since protein may be used to produce energy, if necessary. If there is insufficient energy in the diet either food protein or body protein can be broken down and used in the same way as glucose. This, however, is very wasteful because once it is used for energy, it can not be used for body protein 'repair'.

It is not surprising, therefore, that there is a close relationship between protein and energy requirements; if enough carbohydrate and fat are consumed, protein requirements for players are no greater than for anyone else. Supplementary proteins are often used by sporting people but unlike the protein in food, they are not normally associated with energy – which means that they will not be well used. Work currently in progress at Leeds Polytechnic tends to indicate that the consumption of protein supplements can actually cause some athletes to reduce their overall food intake. This is clearly counter-productive in terms of maintaining an adequate energy and nutrient supply. Finally, it should be stated that protein will *only* be incorporated into muscle tissue if there is an appropriate training programmme.

Amino acids are the tiny molecules which are joined together in particular sequences to make proteins. Proteins in hair will have a different sequence to the proteins in muscle (which is why hair and muscle look so different). Once again all proteins contain all amino acids but in different amounts, depending on source and function. Generally proteins from animal sources are nearer in amino acid pattern and proportion to our own bodies and our needs. However, it is possible to get all these amino acids from plant sources. Vegetarians do this and are perfectly healthy. It is quite possible to rely on the cheaper vegetable sources of protein and, by mixing foods together, a better mix of amino acids is ensured. Putting cereals (bread, pasta, rice) together with nuts or pulses (dried beans, peas or lentils) creates a perfect complement of amino acids precisely the same as that found in the best sirloin!

How Much Protein?

The actual amount one needs is difficult to say. It is possible to give values for grams of protein but this is meaningless unless it is put into the context of food. Values for adults of 1–2g protein per kg of body-weight per day have been given. For someone who weighs 80kg the need for protein could be estimated at 80–160g per day. The values quoted in the DHSS recommended intake tables are comparable to this. About 40 kcals of energy are required per gram of protein. In the above example this would mean a food energy intake of between 3,200 and 6,400 kcals per day.

Food, however, is a mixture of nutrients and if the food in the diet provides, say, 3,000 kcals, then this amount is likely to contain at least 80g of protein and probably a lot more. It is very difficult to consume too little protein when eating a variety of foods (*see* Fig 60).

Making Weight

Consuming extra protein may well be counter-productive, so that the only way of actually gaining appropriate weight is to follow a rigorous and intensive exercise programme which increases the muscle tissue. The energy required to sustain this level of exercise is considerable and it is likely that if muscle is not being laid down it is because the intensity of the exercise is inadequate. The energy for muscular activity is obtained from food and stored in the body as either glycogen or fat. Glycogen is stored in limited amounts and so is probably the major constraint on duration and intensity of exercise. If the dietary energy presented to the body is primarily fat or protein then little glycogen will be stored. In order to make weight the diet should be rich in carbohydrate (see Fig 60), which is generally associated with protein in food. So as the amount of food consumed increases to cover the energy requirements, so the quantity of protein in the diet also automatically increases.

There is little reliable evidence that taking any specific amino acids will miraculously cause an increase in muscle growth. A mixture of amino acids obtained by consuming a good and wide variety of foods will ensure an appropriate balance. You should also remember that protein from eggs, milk, meat and fish could be wasted unless there is an adequate supply of fat and carbohydrate (energy) in the diet as these foods may not be energy rich. It is the dietary CHO and the muscle's glycogen which ultimately influences the intensity of the training. Training is the only means of gaining muscle mass.

MINERALS AND VITAMINS

There is also little evidence to suggest that athletes have a greater bodily demand for vitamins compared to non-athletes. As has been said, food is a mixture of nutrients and as food intake rises (as it must do to support activity) then so does the level of vitamin supply through the food. A very bizarre diet indeed would have to be chosen for any deficiency to occur. However, it is possible to overindulge in vitamin supplements – and this can be dangerous. It is becoming apparent that not only can overindulging in vitamins (even vitamin C) lead to the development of harmful conditions, but also that such supplements affect the absorption of other nutrients. Individuals should take care and if supplements are thought necessary they should seek medical advice to confirm a positive need.

Minerals may be thought of in two groups, those which we require in relatively large amounts and those which we require in trace amounts. The former which are of importance here are sodium, potassium and calcium. Of those required in very small amounts the most important is iron. Sodium and potassium loss in sweat barely reaches levels whereby supplements are required above normal dietary intake and therefore they should not be considered outside the context of a normal varied diet.

There is, however, perhaps slightly more concern over adequate iron intake in athletes, due to the occasional occurrence of the condition known as 'sports anaemia', although it has not been described in Rugby players. The reason for this anaemia is not fully understood and may be a result of physical stress on the red blood cells or from abnormal losses of blood – both due to the intensity and prolonged effort of training and exercise. If anaemia is diagnosed then iron supplements will be advised. It would also be wise to make sure the diet contains iron-rich foods (*see* Fig 60b).

Overall, the athlete who is not restricting intake should not need any supplements of vitamins or minerals. In any event supplements should only be commenced after a deficiency has been confirmed.

TRAINING SCHEDULES AND FOOD FOR COMPETITIONS/MATCHES

Rest periods are a vital part of successful training and allow the player to replenish energy (especially glycogen) and nutrient stores. Any schedule must, of course, allow time for the preparation and consumption of food. Obviously, without food we simply do not have the energy available to perform and it must therefore be an essential part of the training schedule. Indeed it may well be that relaxation periods should become eating periods. 'Tapering' of exercise before a match allows for just this repletion phase. Productivity of training might well be improved if coaches and players were to give more thought to rest and food periods.

Timing of meals should be such that the major part of digestion is complete before activity commences. Fat and protein foods on the whole, take longer to move through the stomach and small intestine (two–four hours). Carbohydrate and cold foods are much quicker (one–two hours, depending upon the size of the meal). Sportsmen and women need to eat after a training session and good anticipation of food needs is essential. As it may not always be possible to consume a full meal, it may be sensible to take your own food (i.e. some sandwiches and a flask of fluid to provide the essential nutrient and fluid replacement). If you do have to eat out then carbohydrate in the form of baked potatoes, pizza or pasta makes the most sensible foods – meals and snacks should always be based on the starchy carbohydrates, since they are more effective at repleting glycogen stores lost through exercise.

TRAINING FOR RUGBY

Training for Rugby, primarily a sport performed under aerobic conditions, mainly aims to enhance the cardiovascular system and muscle. This ensures efficient and continuous supply of 'fuel' and oxygen to the working muscles over a long period. Training sessions at sub-maximal work load – aerobic training – also conditions the body to use its fat stores as the major fuel. This is important, especially under match conditions as the store of fat in the body is much greater than CHO, and will therefore last for longer. However, fat is not the sole fuel and some CHO must also be used; this usage becomes proportionally greater as the intensity of the exercise increases – usually towards the end of a match or training session. It is the reserve of stored CHO present at this time that will determine the duration of intense work. For training sessions that are longer than an hour the amount of stored CHO (glycogen) determines the intensity of the work that the muscles can do. Power becomes increasingly difficult to generate in muscles that have diminishing amounts of available glycogen.

Rugby players need not only stamina to see them through a hard match but also strength for 'explosive' bursts of energy. These bursts demand anaerobic metabolism, when the only fuel source is glucose (glycogen). Training sessions therefore aim both to build muscles and to train them to work and tolerate anaerobic conditions. Each exercise will normally be carried out to exhaustion. This conditions the muscles to anaerobic metabolism and by its nature depletes glycogen.

Training also seems to effect a change in the efficiency with which muscles store glycogen; it has been observed that training brings about swift, efficient repletion of stores, but only if muscles have a plentiful dietary supply. Generally, however, starchy carbohydrate may well be better at replacing the lost glycogen.

Aerobic conditioning requires long training sessions which are also expensive in terms of energy usage; it is therefore essential to take time to eat properly during this training. Concentrated sources of CHO are important (see Fig 60) as well as high energy foods (containing fat) such as chocolate, rich cakes, nuts and biscuits. Drinks or soups are also useful, especially those using milk and adding sugar, eggs or cream. Nor should you forget to replace the fluids which will have been used up in vigorous training.

Rugby players may also need to consider their lean–fat ratio. This consideration of excess body fat is an important part of training, but it is vital that the level of body fat achieved is easily maintained. Constant dieting does little to afford the energy for effective training. Restricting the energy content of the diet should be done by reducing the amount of fat (and foods which contribute high amounts of fat). For example, substitute low-fat spreads for butter or margarine, low-fat milk for full-fat milk, lean cuts of meat or poultry and fish for chops, burgers and sausages and, finally, grill foods rather than fry them. Maintaining the carbohydrate intake will ensure that energy is available to keep to the training schedule. An intense training schedule will also help to burn up excessive body fat. Above all, it is important to find a level of food intake which will enable a constant body-weight to be maintained. Out of season this may be difficult, but when training and playing is reduced, so too must be the amount of food supplied – otherwise body fat will increase. Reducing the amount of fat in the diet is again the easiest way of reducing the energy supply (see Fig 60).

Competition

As competition time approaches, the will to win must be combined with the suggested training programme. Diet can have a role in this but food eaten immediately before a match has little effect on performance; it can in fact be detrimental. It is rather the extended period of preparation, training and diet which will affect performance on the day. Unlike food, it is imperative to drink before a competition since lack of fluids – or dehydration – may prevent you even finishing the match.

How to Arrive Ready to Compete

The message of this chapter has been to ensure that you get the 'energy books balanced', which means ensuring that energy is replaced in the working muscle. If this becomes part of the training schedule then relaxing before the event and allowing the body muscles to recoup their energy reserves takes place quite naturally; that is to say you should 'taper' the training schedule.

In fact, it can be unproductive to follow an unusually high carbohydrate diet for several days before the event, as this can lead to discomfort and diarrhoea. By careful measurement of an athlete's food intake it has been shown how very difficult it is for the individual actually to judge by how much he is increasing his intake. More often than not CHO intake is raised but the contribution to energy intake from fat is lowered, and so the individual is unable to achieve a sufficiently high overall energy intake. This means that instead of the carbohydrate being stored, it may be used for the essential work of body maintenance (so that glycogen storage is less than expected). The message here is that good dietary habits should develop and support training. This will also be highly suitable for immediate preparation for a match (which is often of shorter duration than the training sessions).

The planning of meals and snacks before a match also needs consideration. As already mentioned it is vital to have the intestine as free as possible from the process of digestion; meals should therefore be finished at least two (preferably four) hours before play, since the anticipation of competition may reduce intestinal function. Individuals should carefully plan those meals which they feel will be more beneficial. The content of the meals is largely irrelevant in terms of providing energy, which should have been taken care of 12–48 hours beforehand, although sugary snacks should be avoided as these may delay the release of internal energy (*see* below). It would also be wise to avoid those foods which are known to produce flatulence as this can be very uncomfortable during a match!

There are two factors which affect the utilisation of fuel. Firstly, taking something sugary about forty-five minutes before starting an event will 'catch the body out', as it will be expecting to store food or nutrients and not to mobilise fuel. Moreover, the hormones which act to control body chemistry will not promote energy release, which can be very unfortunate for the athlete about to start a match! Secondly, the type of training will have deter-mined how the individual responds to the demands of the exercise (i.e. whether or not fat is predominantly 'burned', so sparing glycogen).

Once the match has started, however, it is possible to take on some extra fuel in the form of carbohydrate, taken about half an hour into the match (during an injury break or at half-time). This can spare some of the stored glycogen and enable the player to keep going for longer. The form in which this is taken can pose a problem. It needs to be rapidly emptied from the stomach and also to be easily absorbed. Sugary drinks may not leave the stomach rapidly if they are 'hyperosmolar' (a solution of over five per cent is probably too strong). However, a drink containing special sugars called maltodextrins may be much stronger; a solution of twenty per cent can be tolerated. This means that in 100ml (roughly half a glass) there could be as much as 20g of carbohydrate or 80kcal of energy (about the same as a slice of bread). This may not seem to be very much but it has been shown to be effective in endurance events. However, there may still be some slowing of transfer between stomach and intestine so that in hot climates, where the more immediate need is for fluid, plain water or the very dilute solution out-lined above, should be used.

Some ergogenic (or exercise-enhancing) aids may be tried. One which has some use, provided it is not misused by over-indulgence, is caffeine. Con-sumed about forty-five minutes before exercise, it has two effects: firstly, it is a stimulant and reduces the feeling of effort and secondly it causes fatty acids to be 'mobilised' and used as fuel, so sparing glycogen.

The amount of caffeine which has been found to produce this effect is 4mg per kg of body-weight. Caffeine is found in chocolate to a small extent and in drinks in the following amounts:

1 cup (200ml) cola		35mg
1 cup (150ml) coffee, instant		70mg
	percolated	120mg
	filter	160mg
1 cup (150ml) tea		50mg

Caffeine is a drug. If it is given in large and uncontrolled amounts it can pro-duce vascular changes which are harmful. In addition, at everyday doses it can have a pronounced diuretic effect which is undesirable when hydration is required.

Indeed hydration is probably the single most important factor for success on the day. It is essential that fluid is replaced as often as possible during the match. This is not very easy in Rugby, but advantage should be taken whenever the opportunity arises (such as during an injury break or at half-time). The concept of fluid with a suitable concentration to ensure maximum absorption has been discussed earlier.

Summary

Eating for Rugby should become part of the training schedule. Eating food which will support intense training, body musculature and hard match play is a key to success. The monitoring of food is therefore of the utmost importance and should form an integral part of the schedule. Every Rugby player should be aware of the necessity for adequate hydration.

4   Injury Prevention

CLASSIFICATION OF INJURY

In order to prevent injuries it is preferable to understand why they occur and where they occur in the body. An injury may be due to an external force (extrinsic injury) or to a force within the body (intrinsic injury). Extrinsic injuries happen when a player collides with an object such as the uprights, the ground or another player. They can also be caused by an object hitting the body such as the ball. Intrinsic injuries may happen without any particular cause (incidental injury) but they are more likely to occur when the training load is rapidly increased in intensity and frequency (overuse injury). Most injuries tend to occur quite suddenly (acute injury), but fortunately tend to settle very quickly. However, an acute injury may become chronic, which is usually more difficult to treat and takes longer to overcome. You are far more likely to get injured towards the end of a training session or match, when you become tired, than at any other time, so take more care as you become fatigued.

SITE OF INJURY

Sports injuries may occur anywhere in the body, such as in muscles, tendons (pullies attached to the bone from the muscles), tenosynovia (the protective sheaths around a tendon), ligaments (fibrous bands joining two bones together at a joint), joints and bones. It is helpful to grade the injuries into three groups:

(i)   Group A   Minimal damage when only bruising occurs and there is no major disruption to the muscle, tendon, ligament or whatever. Small blood vessels are damaged, however, and leak blood which forms a bruise (haematoma).

(ii)   Group B   Some disruption of the tissues takes place and a sprain, strain, partial tear or partial rupture takes place in a muscle, tendon (tendonitis), tendon sheath (tenosynovitis), ligament or bone (stress fracture). Stress fractures of bones can be likened to the cracks in a piece of wire which has been repeatedly bent, at first the wire looks strong but eventually, if stressed enough, it can break right through.

(iii)   Group C   Complete ruptures of muscles, tendons, and ligaments, fractured or broken bones and dislocated joints.

Further classification of injury can be as shown below:

Extrinsic (outside force)
  collisions
  falls
  equipment

Intrinsic (internal force)
  incidental (no cause)
  overuse
  acute
  chronic

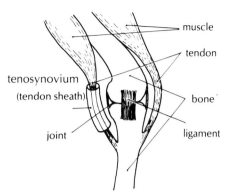

Fig 62   *Physiological representation of the knee.*

AVOIDANCE OF INJURIES

The basic rule for avoiding injury is to increase your own fitness through increased speed, strength, endurance and flexibility, as outlined in Chapter 2. Using the training programme in a sensible, progressive way reduces the chances of sustaining intrinsic and overuse injuries. Skill is not only important in making a better all-round player but also enables him to avoid injury through inappropriate technique. Tackling and being tackled account for almost half of the extrinsic injuries in Rugby, so it is important to teach and practise good tackling technique, always avoiding head-on contact. The front-row forwards are in the most dangerous position in the scrum, so good binding, avoiding collapse, avoiding violent wheeling and decreasing the impact when forming a set scrum will all reduce the number of neck injuries.

Warm-Up and Cool-Down

Warm-up is essential not only in preparation for matches but also in training. By gradually increasing the intensity of work and building up the number of skills to be rehearsed the body and mind are both being warmed up (*see* Chapter 2). The muscles are controlled by electrical impulses fed to them from the brain and this system needs tuning and adjusting – just as the muscles need warming up. Equally important is the cool-down, when more emphasis is put on flexibility in order to test for any minor injury that may have occurred during exercise.

Gentle rhythmic movement also helps in flushing out the waste products of metabolism from the muscles that build up during high intensity exercise. Muscle stiffness the following day can be reduced by performing a regular post-match or post-training drill of stretching and low-intensity exercise (*see* Chapter 2).

Protection

Most extrinsic injuries can be avoided by taking sensible precautions – such as checking the safety of the training venue and any equipment that is used in it. Gyms should be well ventilated, well lit and with any sharp edges, radiators or nearby walls padded with foam. Doors and windows should be secured and other recreational equipment stored correctly and well out of the way of the training area.

The pitch should be checked before each match or training session (and especially carefully at the beginning of the season) to make sure no sharp stones, glass or metal objects have been left on the grass. The uprights should be padded and the touch flags must be easily knocked over when hit. Weight-training equipment should only be used under supervision and all users should be familiar with the safety procedures.

The ball should be of the approved type; heavy balls may cause injuries to the fingers, wrists and forearms while children may need to start with lighter, smaller, plastic balls. Your clothing should be well fitting, not too tight (causing abrasions) nor too loose (restricting free movement) and tops should be long-sleeved to prevent friction burns.

Gum shields not only protect your teeth but also reduce the chance of more serious jaw injury and concussion by dissipating the energy of a blow to the chin. Your ears should be protected with tape if you play in the scrum and front-row forwards can reduce leg injuries by wearing shin-pads. Boots should be well fitting; wear new boots for short periods in training only until they feel comfortable – this will help to prevent blisters. You should always remove dentures and on no account should you ever chew gum when either training or playing.

Some players may wish to strap their fingers, ankles or feet, particularly if they have been injured in the past. The strapping must not be elastic so that the joints are adequately supported and must be removed after exercise, allowing a full range of movement to take place. A trained physiotherapist can show you how to apply the tape.

Self-Control

The rules of the game and the regulations controlling the use of training venues have been devised not only to ensure fair play but also to prevent injury; it is therefore prudent to observe these rules for your own safety. It is especially important in Rugby to play with and against people of your own physique and standard of play. Many serious neck injuries have occurred in people playing against much stronger opposition.

The tactics of the set and loose play need to be learned and rehearsed with the coach and other players in order to reach a better understanding with your own team. Self-control also plays an important role in preventing and reducing injury. Try to organise your day so that there is adequate time for meals, allowing at least two hours to elapse after a large meal before training (*see* Chapter 3). Most athletes need a minimum of eight hours sleep each night and time must also be allocated for training, eating, studying or working. Fatigue will set in if not enough time is allowed for adequate rest between training sessions and this is the biggest cause of most sports injuries as well as skill breakdown.

Regular showering or bathing after training and frequent washing of kit will help reduce the incidence of fungal infections of the skin. Do not borrow other people's clothing or towels and make sure you always have clean, dry clothing to change into after a training session. Athletes should be non-smokers not only for obvious health reasons but also because the nicotine in cigarettes attaches itself to the oxygen-carrying component of the red blood cells (haemoglobin) thus reducing the available space for oxygen to be transported to the muscles. This effect lasts for up to three weeks after the last cigarette has been smoked.

By tradition many Rugby players drink alcohol not only after but some-times before a match! Alcohol should never be consumed before a match or training session – not only to avoid errors of judgement but also because alcohol dehydrates the body and makes the body perform less efficiently. After a hard match or training session, particularly if it is hot, plain fluid should be drunk first before racing to the bar.

Check-List for Injury Prevention

(i)   Environment: clothes; shoes; equipment; surfaces.
(ii)   Control: training/match rules; physique; tactics.
(iii)   Fitness: skill; strength; speed; endurance; flexibility.
(iv)   Self-discipline: warm-up; diet; sleep; smoking; hygiene.

MEDICAL PROBLEMS

Frequently it may be illness and not injury that prevents the sportsperson from training. Any Rugby player who has an infection, such as a heavy cold, a chest infection or flu, should not train or play, especially if the body temperature is elevated above normal (36.9°C, 98.4°F), or if the resting pulse rate is appreciably higher than normal. You will not be able to perform well and certainly will not get any beneficial training affect if you continue to train at this stage; you also run the risk of the infection getting worse and the heart muscle being affected (myocarditis). Rest is essential until the illness passes. Low-grade chronic infections of the teeth, skin or sinuses, for example, may prevent you performing at peak level and treatment should be sought earlier rather than later. Some virus infections such as glandular fever may linger on for weeks and regrettably there is no treatment – so you must remain patient until the illness passes, returning gradually to full training. Every player should be protected against tetanus and have a booster injection every ten years.

Dehydration

A reduction in body-weight of one per cent through sweat results in a ten per cent reduction in work capacity; likewise a two per cent loss will result in a twenty per cent reduction in work capacity. It is therefore vital that any sweat lost is adequately and promptly replaced by water, not only to enhance performance, but also to prevent injury. Some people (particularly when training regularly in the summer, or end of the summer, in hot gyms) may become chronically dehydrated with a subsequent reduction in body-weight, reduced urine output and a rise in resting pulse. Regular weighing and checking of the volume and colour of the urine should ensure that dehydration does not become a problem (thirst alone is not a reliable indicator of dehydration).

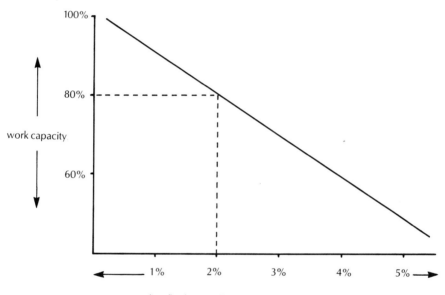

Example: 2% lost fluid = 20% reduction in work capacity

Fig 63 The relationship between the loss of body fluid and reduction in work capacity.

OVERTRAINING

This condition is difficult to spot and may creep up on the player and coach without either being aware of what is happening. It usually occurs when the player increases the training load both in frequency and intensity, not allowing enough time to eat, sleep, study or work. As the performance drops off the athlete tries to compensate by increasing the training load only to suffer further deterioration in performance, starting down the slippery slope and getting involved in a vicious circle of increased work and poor performance. The only cure is to rest for four days and increase both the fluid and carbohydrate intake, resisting the temptation to restart training after only one or two days when feeling a little recovered.

WOMEN

Women who have frequent heavy periods may lose enough iron to make themselves anaemic. When anaemia occurs the red blood cells are unable to carry sufficient oxygen to the muscles, resulting in tiredness both on and off the pitch. The doctor can easily correct this deficiency and advice should be sought as early as possible. Some women who undergo a lot of endurance training may cease to have periods, particularly if they reduce their body fat. This condition is known as amenorrhoea and is quite normal in these circumstances; periods will return when the training load is decreased. Pregnant women can safely continue to train until they start feeling uncomfortable, indeed regular exercise in pregnancy results in healthier babies and easier childbirth for the mother. Playing competitive games, however, is best avoided in order to decrease the risk of miscarriage from body contact.

CHILDREN

Bones continue to grow up to the age of about eighteen in males and sixteen in females. However, during growth the bones are not strong enough for the muscles and tendons attached to them, so heavy weight-training and repetitive high-load training should not be performed by pre-pubertal children. In some children the points at which tendons are attached to bones become inflamed, swollen and tender. This may happen just below the knee (Osgood–Schlatter's condition) or at the back of the heel (Sever's condition). The only treatment is to reduce the loading to that particular point by cutting down on the training until the condition settles.

Children can train on resilient surfaces such as grass and during training the use of shock-absorbing heel inserts made of sorbothane will prove effective in relieving pain. Children develop power and explosive force after puberty and so power training should not be undertaken until after this time. Training with very light weights will, however, help with the technical skills of heavier weight-training later on.

VETERANS

Older sportspeople are not especially prone to particular injuries, but as age advances, the chance of their being injured increases and the longer it takes them to recover from injury. If you go back to Rugby, having had a few years away from sport, start gently with a gradual increase in the frequency and intensity of each session. Secondary injuries may occur in joints previously damaged in earlier years; for example, an injury such as osteoarthritis of the knee joint may develop long after a torn cartilage has been removed. These secondary injuries may prevent you from doing as much training as you would like, but you will have to adjust to this, perhaps supplementing your usual training with swimming and cycling.

TRAVEL

When travelling away from home, whether abroad or in your own country, you may experience difficulty in sleeping especially during the first few nights. A muscle relaxant may prove helpful at this time and your doctor should be able to help if it becomes a problem. Stay clear of new and untried exotic foods, keep to your usual diet if at all possible and wash any fruit or salads in *clean* water before eating them. Check that the water supply is safe to drink and if not, consume bottled water only. When going to a hot climate the body takes ten days or so to acclimatise to the heat. After this period the salt content of the sweat is reduced and stabilised so all that is required is a little extra salt during the first few days, although you should not take salt tablets which can make you feel ill.

If you have a fair skin, you should keep out of the sun, and even if you tan easily you should still avoid sunbathing as you may become dehydrated. Ideally you should always wear long sleeves and long trousers at dusk and at dawn to avoid insect bites and should also use plenty of insect repellent. Check with your doctor to find out whether any special vaccinations are required well in advance of your trip. A travel check-list will include: vaccinations; food; water; heat acclimatisation; sleep disturbance; jet lag.

DOPING

It is your responsibility as a player to ensure that you do not abuse drug-testing regulations, either intentionally or by error. Mistakes can occur when over-the-counter pain killers, cough mixtures, anti-diarrhoea medicines and nasal decongestants are used which may contain small amounts of codeine and ephedrine. Both drugs are on the banned list and will show up in urine as a positive dope test. Check with the governing body or the Sports Council's Drugs Advisory Group for an up-to-date list of drugs you can and cannot take.

FIRST AID

Resuscitation

If you are a coach you have a responsibility to know the basic procedures of resuscitation. When a serious casualty occurs your first aim is to save life before worrying about the extent of any sports injury:

(i)   Check the airway and remove any object which might be preventing air entering the lungs; remove any false teeth or mouth guards, clear the mouth of vomit or chewing gum and loosen any clothing around the throat. Extend the neck fully in order to prevent the tongue flopping down against the back of the throat.

(ii)   Check that the casualty is now breathing; if not, start CPR (cardio-pulmonary resuscitation) by giving the kiss of life. Breath into the mouth of the casualty at the same time as pinching his or her nose to prevent air escaping from it.

(iii)   Check the circulation by feeling for a pulse; if you cannot detect it, start compressing the chest wall firmly four times for each of your breaths until the casualty starts breathing and regains his or her pulse, or until the ambulance arrives.

(iv)   After the patient has regained consciousness or started breathing by him or herself, check for any bleeding. If there is bleeding, apply firm pressure with a gauze swab or handkerchief for five minutes (in most cases this will be sufficient to stop blood loss from major blood vessels). You can then start assessing the extent of any injury and try to relieve pain by placing the casualty in a stable position on their side, splinting any obvious fractures. Ideally you should always have checked beforehand where the nearest telephone is; you must then send someone to summon the ambulance in order to evacuate the injured person.

Treatment of Sports Injuries

The aim of treatment is to reduce the amount of damage already done, relieve pain and promote healing. When a sports injury or soft-tissue injury occurs, small blood vessels become torn and blood escapes causing bruising and swelling. Actions should be taken to help reduce the amount of blood escaping and so cut down on the size of the swelling, both of which hinder repair and rehabilitation. A mnemonic (RICE) is useful in this context.

Rest
Ice
Compression
Elevation

Rest is required for the first twenty-four hours following an injury in order to prevent further bleeding.

Ice is applied to the injury for ten minutes every two hours in the first twenty-four hours. This reduces pain, swelling and further bleeding. The ice should be wrapped in a damp tea-towel and must not come into direct contact with the skin; if it does an ice burn may occur. If ice is not available, cold water from the tap will suffice, as will a bag of frozen peas from the freezer!

Compression of the injury by a firmly applied crêpe bandage prevents further blood loss and reduces the size of any swelling. The bandage should not be too tight and you may need to reapply the crêpe in the first twenty-four hours if it becomes too loose or too tight.

Elevation assists in the 'drainage' of swelling and the prevention of further loss of blood. The affected limb should be raised above the level of the heart for twenty-four hours.

Treatment of Blisters

The treatment for blisters depends upon whether or not the skin overlying it is intact. If it is, the blister should be left well alone but if the skin has been broken the blister should be 'deroofed' with a clean pair of scissors. This prevents infection setting in and also assists in the blister bed healing more rapidly, if perhaps a little more uncomfortably in the short term. While training, the blister should be covered with a dry, non-absorbent dressing, held in place by a piece of tape or strapping. While on the subject of first aid, the contents of any first-aid box should include: crêpe bandages; gauze squares; zinc oxide tape; plasters; cotton wool; triangular bandage; scissors; antiseptic solution; analgesic (pain-killing) tablets; collar; splints. You should also have access to a stretcher, blanket and Brooks airway.

REHABILITATION

Early rehabilitation of most injuries should be encouraged in order to shorten the time taken to reach a full recovery. In the first twenty-four hours when 'RICE' is applied, gentle passive movements are made to assist in the drainage of any swelling and to prevent blood clots forming in the deep veins. After a further twenty-four hours, more active stretching exercises are performed followed by strengthening exercises. The muscles around an injury rapidly lose power and the co-ordination of muscle movements also worsens within a few hours of the injury being sustained. As the muscles regain power, re-education of Rugby skills becomes a priority, eventually allowing a return to training and to playing matches.

Models for Rehabilitation

Group A injuries.

Bruising only has occurred and all that is generally required is the application of RICE in the first twenty-four hours followed by a fairly rapid resumption of normal training.

Group B injuries.

Ligaments/joints. A sprained ligament on the outside of the ankle joint is one of the most common Rugby injuries. The principles used for the rehabilitation of this particular injury may also be applied to similar injuries to other parts of the body.

After the first twenty-four hours (when RICE is applied) you should try to walk on the injured side without a limp in order to stretch any scar tissue that is forming into its correct anatomical alignment. Initially this may mean that you will have to walk very slowly, before progressing first to normal walking pace and then to walking and jogging on grass five to ten metres at a time, slowly increasing the distance to twenty-five, fifty, seventy-five and then one hundred metres. When you have reached this stage, continue jogging for up to four hundred metres before starting a few sprints of five to ten metres followed by sprints of twenty-five, fifty, seventy-five and one hundred metres. Now run backwards and start weaving and jumping to strengthen the ankle further. Now start dribbling a soccer ball and then begin to kick the ball further and further, working towards a full kick. If you can do this, repeat the procedure using a Rugby ball, dribbling, kicking and punting.

Nerves are damaged in a ligament injury and so lose their ability to tell the brain where in space the foot is. These nerves need to be re-educated and the best way to do so is by doing balance exercises. These positional or 'proprioceptive' exercises must be done at the same time as the stretching and strengthening drills. Start by trying to 'stork-stand' on your injured leg and then close your eyes. After this try throwing a ball up into the air and catching it again while still balancing on one leg. The degree of difficulty can be increased by standing on a balance or wobble board. When you can do all of this quite happily for fifteen to twenty minutes you are then fit enough to resume normal training with your squad or team. However, if having done this your ankle still does not feel stable or if you are unable to play, you should seek advice from a sports clinic or qualified physiotherapist.

Muscles and tendons. Torn thigh muscles (quadriceps) may occur in Rugby when jumping vigorously for the ball or landing awkwardly from a jump. The aim of rehabilitation is to prevent shortening of the muscle or tendon by inappropriate scar tissue formation (scar tissue may contract for several weeks after an injury).

Following the usual RICE application in the first twenty-four hours you should gently stretch the quadriceps muscle each morning and evening and for a minute every hour during the day. As gentle stretching becomes less uncomfortable, more active stretching and static strengthening exercises should be undertaken followed by dynamic exercises with increased loadings. Accordingly, start with straight-leg exercises, then bend the knee, and then add weights of one to two kilograms attached to the ankle while bending and straightening the knee.

After this the routine of jogging, sprinting, weaving, running backwards and dribbling a ball, together with balance exercises (as used for the ankle injury) should be followed.

Group C injuries.

Bone fractures and dislocated joints. Most fractures or broken bones, together with joint dislocations are major injuries and will need a minimum of six weeks' immobilisation before any rehabilitation can commence. They also require close medical supervision. Stress fractures, however, need only to be rested for three weeks before gentle progressive training is resumed. If you think you have a stress fracture you should stop training and seek medical advice.

Concussion

If a player is concussed (in other words has lost consciousness – however briefly – with or without memory loss) he or she must stop immediately and be examined by a doctor or sent to the nearest casualty department. The. player should not be allowed to play again for *three weeks.* If he or she is unfortunate enough to be concussed again the period should be extended to six weeks and if the player is concussed for a third time in the same season, he or she should not play again for four months.

5   Mental Training

It is ironic that despite the widespread recognition of mental factors in sport, very few practical training books on specific sports make more than a passing reference to mental training. Nevertheless, there are now quite a few books on mental training in sport, some of which are listed in Further Reading at the end of this book. The complete player will be someone who trains physically *and* mentally!

In his book entitled *The Pursuit of Sporting Excellence* (1986) David Hemery recalls his numerous interviews with a wide range of sport's highest achievers. In response to his question, 'to what extent was the mind involved in playing your sport?', he reported that 'the unanimous verdict was couched in words like "immensely", "totally", "that's the whole game", "you play with your mind", "that's where the body movement comes from" '. Barry John said he was always 'looking to make things happen' and that it had to do with 'his temperament and inner belief'. In short, we all recognise the importance of having the right mental approach in sport just as we recognise the importance of physical factors. The purpose of this chapter, therefore, is to present a selection of some mental training skills relevant to Rugby players (in fact many of the skills are relevant to most people in a wide variety of sports). Before outlining some of these skills, it is important to dispel some of the myths surrounding mental training in sport.

MYTHS AND TRUTHS

Myth 1   'You only need a sports psychologist if you have mental problems.' If that was the case then, extending the argument, we would only need to train physically when we were trying to recover from injury! There is no difference between practising physical and mental skills – they should both be practised regularly as a positive aid to performance and not just to offset 'problems' (although they can usefully be employed for this as well).

Myth 2   'All good athletes have a natural mental toughness and don't need to practise mental skills.' Certainly some people will have better mental qualities than others (in exactly the same way that some people are more physically gifted than others) but that does not mean that mental training will not help. Even players like Gareth Edwards, John Kirwin and Dean Richards have put in tremendous amounts of physical training even though they are clearly physically gifted people. These days natural ability is not enough.

Myth 3 'Mental skills cannot be trained or developed.' This is similar to the last myth, and it, too, is incorrect. All skills, whether physical or mental can be improved with appropriate practice.

Mental training may not be fully accepted by all people in sport, but it is hoped that the preceding argument may have convinced you that it is illogical to expect physical training to be the only type of sports training when we all recognise that many games are won and lost on mental attitudes and abilities. Many years ago it was considered slightly odd – even 'unsporting' – to train more than about three days a week. That attitude has long since gone but has been replaced with a reluctance to accept regular mental training as a part of contemporary sport. In a few years time, perhaps, we will look back at such an odd attitude with a sense of amusement!

COMPONENTS OF MENTAL TRAINING

In Chapter 2 the various components of physical fitness-training were outlined and it was stated then that fitness was best defined in terms of its constituent parts. In the same way, it would be naive to say that mental training is made up of just one factor. It is a term given to a number of different components, but it will not be possible to cover all of these in detail in such a short space and interested readers are referred to Further Reading at the back of this book. What will be done here, however, is to outline the basic features of five topics, which are:

(i)   Relaxation and the control of stress.
(ii) Mental imagery.
(iii) Concentration and mental control.
(iv) Self-confidence.
(v)   Team-work.

The background to each of these areas will be explained in brief, including examples from Rugby, and then some practical mental training exercises in each area will be outlined. However, it should be noted that not all mental skills can be easily taught by coaches without training – although the exercises outlined here have been chosen for simplicity and safety. It is recommended, however, that if mental exercises are introduced, they are first done so by a registered sports psychologist of the British Association of Sports Sciences (*see* Useful Addresses). Coaches are also advised to attend courses on sports psychology run by the National Coaching Foundation (whose address is also at the end of the book).

Relaxation and the Control of Stress

Relaxation is a much misunderstood concept in mental training, many players thinking that if relaxation skills are needed at all, they are only needed before a game. Clearly, being too relaxed is not a good idea, nor is being too tense. The answer, therefore, is to control the 'on–off switch' of the body. On most radios the on–off switch also controls the volume. As we are 'on' all of the time, the essence of controlling the on–off switch is to control the volume. One way to do this is to learn relaxation skills, of which there are many. Other mental skills, such as mental imagery and concentration, are also dependent upon being able to control the relaxation and activation (arousal) of the body.

Relaxation not only facilitates rest and recovery in sport, but can also have a more immediate effect on performance through reducing anxiety and muscle tension. Moreover, this can relate to self-confidence – another mental skill to be discussed later.

Arousal is the 'intensity-aspect' of our behaviour since we often refer to being under-aroused (e.g. drowsy, sleepy) or over-aroused (e.g. over-excited, panicky). In sport it is easy to get over-aroused with the excitement of the situation, for example the Rugby player who is so 'psyched-up' at the kick-off that he charges down the field only to discover that he has over-run the ball by thirty metres! This shows that over-arousal is not necessarily a good thing in sport and can badly affect concentration.

There are many different types of relaxation skill that can be learned, including breathing exercises, muscle tense–relax exercises and meditation. After a time, you will develop your own preference and there is no one technique that can be recommended more than another. Two techniques will be outlined here, and others can be found in the books listed in the Further Reading. It should be recognised that not everyone is suited to starting these exercises especially those with abnormal blood pressure, a history of cardiorespiratory health problems, asthmatics, and those suffering acute anxiety states, who should all be referred to their doctor beforehand.

Deep Muscle Relaxation

This simple technique requires you to lie on the floor with your arms and legs stretched out. Gradually reduce your breathing rate to a slow yet comfortable rate, start saying the word 'relax' to yourself as you breathe out. Close your eyes when you feel ready to do so, but do not force it. After about ten exhalations, coupled with the word 'relax', focus your attention on your left leg. Imagine it getting gradually heavier and heavier as you become increasingly relaxed. Imagine your leg sinking into the mat (concentrate on this for about a minute). Now shift your attention to your right leg and repeat the exercise. This can also be done for your left and right arms in succession. After this you should be quite relaxed and feeling 'heavy' – with little or no muscular tension. Slowly sit up, stretch and return to normal activities.

This should be practised for short spells initially as your concentration is likely to be poor. Five minutes may not sound very much but will be long enough for the first session. This form of deep relaxation is best performed several hours before competition to allow you plenty of time to increase the arousal level to the appropriate point for the match.

Progressive Muscle Relaxation

Progressive muscle relaxation (PMR) is a well-known technique for learning the difference between relaxation and tension. It was developed in the 1930s by Edmund Jacobson and is widely used in sport, health and other contexts today. Essentially, the technique is built upon the premise that you will be unable to relax effectively until you can first recognise tension. Consequently, the exercises are a series of tense–relax exercises designed to increase the awareness of muscular tension and relaxation, as illustrated in Fig 64. Below there is a PMR script which you can either have read to you or it can be recorded in a quiet, relaxed voice.

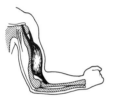 

Fig 64   The tense-relax sequence of progressive muscle relaxation.

Relaxation Procedures

These procedures should be practised twice a day for about ten minutes at a time (evenings are often a good time to practise). The order of the steps involved is very important; however, the particular words or thoughts that the athlete uses to accomplish each step are not. For example, it is important that you relax prior to concentrating on bowling. When you are concentrating on relaxing your arms, we don't care if you say to yourself, 'Now I am going to release all the muscular tension in my hands, fingers, and forearms,' or if you say, 'Now I am going to relax the muscles in my hands, fingers, and arms.'

Prior to beginning the exercise, find a quiet, comfortable place where you will not be disturbed and where you can either sit or lie down. If you wear contact lenses, you may want to remove them. If you have on restrictive clothing (like a tie), you may want to loosen it. Make yourself comfortable with your hands at your sides or in your lap and you are ready to begin.

1   Close your eyes and take three deep breaths, inhaling and exhaling

deeply and slowly. As you exhale, relax your entire body as much as you can. Continue to notice your breathing throughout the session. You will find that as you exhale, your relaxation will become deeper.

2   Now clench both of your fists. Close them and squeeze them tighter and tighter together. As you squeeze them, notice the tension in your forearms, your hands, and your fingers. That's fine, now let them go, relax them. Let your fingers become loose and notice the pleasant feeling of heaviness in your arms and hands as the tension disappears. Feel the heaviness of your arms and hands as they rest against your body or the chair. That's fine, try it one more time, clench both fists and feel the tension, squeeze harder, hold the tension, now let go and completely relax.

3   Now bend your elbows, clench your fists, and flex your biceps. Flex them harder, hold the tension and study it. Now unbend your elbows, relax your hands, get your arms back in a comfortable position, study how your arms feel as you completely let go and relax them.

4   Now straighten your arms and flex the triceps muscle in the back of your upper arms. Hold the tension, increase it, squeeze harder, study the tension. That's fine, now relax, return your arms to a comfortable position and enjoy the release from the tension. Enjoy the feelings, and even when you feel completely relaxed, try and let go even more.

5   Now clench your teeth, feel the muscles tightening in your neck and jaws. Once again, study the tension, clench your teeth tighter, tighter. Now relax your jaws, let your mouth open slightly, and feel your muscles loosen, feel the relief from the tension.

6   Pay attention to your neck muscles. Press your head back as far as it will go and feel the tension, now roll it straight to the right. Again feel the increase in the tension in your muscles. Move your head to the left, pressing hard and feeling the tension in your muscles. Hold the same position and study the tension. Now let your head move into a comfortable position and relax the muscles in your neck and shoulders. Notice the pleasant change as you feel the tension leaving your muscles. Pay attention to how your neck and shoulders feel when the muscles are relaxed.

7   Now pay attention to your breathing and relax your entire body. Breathe deeply and slowly, and as you exhale, relax all the muscles in your arms. Just let yourself go and completely relax. Let your mouth open slightly and relax the muscles in your face, jaw, and forehead. Relax the muscles in your neck and shoulders . . . Relax the muscles in your feet, your calves, and your thighs . . . That's fine . . . just completely relax and let yourself go. Continue to breathe deeply and slowly, and enjoy the pleasant feeling of being completely relaxed.

8   At this time those of you who wish may practise rehearsing the sights and feelings that you associate with a particular pleasant activity. This practice should not last for more than four to five minutes.

9   Now, since you have relaxed so completely, it is best to take your time in moving around. Get out of this relaxed state by using three steps. First, count one and take a deep breath and hold it. Second, count two and stretch your arms and legs, then exhale. Third, count three and open your eyes. You should be wide awake and feeling very relaxed and comfortable.

Procedure Summary
1   Close your eyes and breathe deeply and slowly.
2   Relax the muscles in your forearms.
3   Relax your biceps.
4   Relax your triceps.
5   Relax your face, jaw, and forehead.
6   Relax your neck and shoulders.
7   Breathe slowly and relax your entire body.
8   Rehearse an activity.
9   Take a deep breath, stretch, and open your eyes.

These relaxation procedures are reprinted with permission from Nideffer, R.M., *The Inner Athlete* (Thomas Y. Crowell, 1976).

It is also possible to purchase relaxation tapes (available from the National Coaching Foundation). Fig 65 shows some of the exercises for PMR.

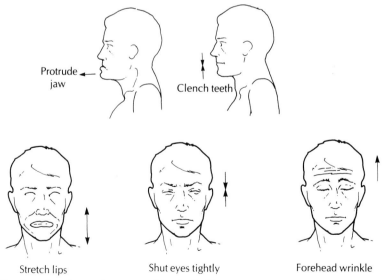

Fig 65   Exercises for tension recognition in PMR.

Shoulders down-reach

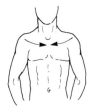

Chin compress on to neck

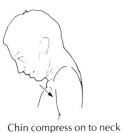

Press head on to mat

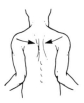

Shoulder blades (back)

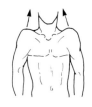

Shoulder blades (forward)

Shoulder blades (up)

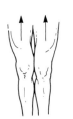

Thighs contract

Buttocks contract

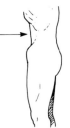

Stomach compress

Prayer arm-push

Toe-curl (back)

Toe-curl (under)

Ankle (back)

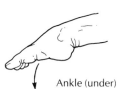

Ankle (under)

Knees press

Fig 65 Continued.

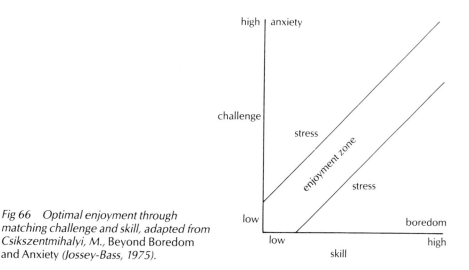

Fig 66 Optimal enjoyment through matching challenge and skill, adapted from Csikszentmihalyi, M., Beyond Boredom and Anxiety (Jossey-Bass, 1975).

Relaxation, Anxiety and Stress

We have all experienced the unpleasantness of anxiety in sport; the nervousness before a big game, or the critical point in the match which could swing it either way. However, not all stress is bad. Stress actually refers to any situation when we are 'out of balance', such as when the task appears to be too difficult or too easy for us. (The latter will produce the stress of boredom, hence the diagram in Fig 66 which shows that optimum enjoyment is often the result of matching the challenge with the right level of skills; any imbalance could cause stress.) The body prepares for stress through the 'fight–flight' reaction, which is the response of the body preparing for action with increased heart rate, breathing rate, adrenalin flow and so on. This feeling could equally be fear or excitement, depending upon how you see the situation. If you hear footsteps rapidly approaching you from behind in a dark alleyway late at night you will react with fear if you think it is a mugger. However, if you think it is a jogger you will not react in the same way. In other words, your stress or anxiety response depends upon the way in which you see the situation. In Rugby, you will need to develop relaxation skills and a positive way of looking at the game whenever you become anxious. In fact, it is quite possible that the pre-match 'psych-up' may cause unnecessary stress to some players; not only will people have different 'psych-up' strategies from each other, but some are also more prone to be 'over-psyched' than others. Although it is common practice in Rugby, greater thought should perhaps be given as to whether it is an appropriate strategy for all players.

Mental Imagery

The ability to visualise events and skills in Rugby is another important mental skill which needs practice. It has been known for some time from psychology experiments that practising a skill mentally is better than not practising at all, although obviously the best course of action is to combine physical with mental practice. But what is mental imagery?

Mental imagery is the repetition of a physical skill or movement sequence that is practised through thought and through pictures, rather than through actual physical movement. Although the exact reasons for why mental imagery works are still not clearly understood, we do know that it works. Experiments as long ago as the 1930s demonstrated that small electrical impulses could be detected in the muscles from thought alone. This suggests that the 'grooving in' of technique in sport can be accomplished, at least in part, by mental imagery. Obviously, such repetitive practice can only take place for predictable skills, such as kicking and some passing skills. Although the situation may change each time in actuality, the general parameters of the skill remain the same. Equally, any set moves can be mentally rehearsed to aid memory. It is more difficult, of course, to rehearse mentally the spontaneous movements that occur in an open team game such as Rugby. However, by visualising such open play and the options and decisions that you may take in such situations your confidence may well be developed.

Brent Rushall, a sports psychologist, lists six important guidelines for successful mental rehearsal in his book, *Psyching in Sport:*

(i)   Your picture should be in the real environment. In other words, if you are wanting to practise a scrum-half pass in a game then imagine yourself passing in a competitive situation − it is more realistic.

(ii)   Perform the skill in full.

(iii) Make sure the visualisation is successful − avoid rehearsing errors (although this is easier said than done!). With practice, though, you should improve the clarity of your mental image and find it easier to control.

(iv)   Visualise the skill before actual performance.

(v)   Imagine the skill at the normal speed.

(vi)   Imagine the skill visually and kinesthetically. In other words, try to feel the movement as if actually performing it. This is best done by visualising yourself actually performing rather than apparently watching yourself on a video. More useful advice can be found in John Syer and Christopher Connolly's book *Sporting Body, Sporting Mind.* They suggest that visualisation should follow these guidelines:

(i)   Start with relaxation.

(ii)   Stay alert.

(iii) Use the present tense.

(iv)   Set realistic and specific goals (*see* later in this chapter).

(v)   Use all of your senses.

(vi)   Visualise at the correct speed.

(vii) Practise regularly.

(viii) Enjoy it!

	Yes	In Between	No
(i) Could you 'see' and 'feel' yourself perform the skill?			
(ii) Could you control the picture?			
(iii) Was the picture clear?			
(iv) Was the skill executed successfully?			
(v) Was the skill at normal speed?			
(vi) Did you stay relaxed?			
(vii) Did you stay alert?			
(viii) Did you use senses other than just 'sight' and 'feel'?			

Fig 67   Mental imagery questionnaire. Answer the questions after each of your initial training sessions with mental imagery. This is based on work by Lew Hardy and John Fazey in The Coach at Work *(National Coaching Foundation, 1986).*

Answer the questionnaire in Fig 67 after your initial attempts at mental imagery. This should highlight some of your problem areas for you to concentrate on next time. Remember, keep the initial sessions short and relax beforehand.

Concentration and Mental Control

We all recognise the importance of concentration but rarely actually practise it as a skill. Try this exercise now but before doing so ensure that you have space around you — for example, make sure there is no furniture that you could hit if you fall over! (Also, it is best to have someone with you just in case you do start to fall over!)

(i)   Stand upright with hands on hips, eyes looking forward. Now take one foot off the ground and rest it against the other shin. How long can you keep your balance without moving the foot that is in contact with the ground?

(ii)   Try the same exercise again, this time with your eyes closed. How long can you keep your balance this time?

(iii)   Finally, try it again, but this time close the eyes and tip the head back. How long can you keep your balance now?

It is probable that your balance deteriorated as you tried these exercises in turn. But why? These exercises each required concentration to maintain balance, but they became more difficult because they gave you less to concentrate on each time. The first exercise allowed you to have your eyes open, so balance was maintained by concentrating on a combination of seeing and feeling, and that is not very difficult because it is the way we operate in normal life. In the second exercise you were deprived of sight and so only had feeling to help you. If you did not concentrate totally on the small deviations of balance, you probably fell. Finally, in the last variation, the balance mechanisms (in the inner ear) were disturbed by tilting your head back and so – unless you could concentrate superbly on the limited feedback you were getting – you easily lost your balance.

What these exercises illustrate is that in sport, concentration is the ability to focus on the details around you that are needed for the game and to exclude those which are extraneous. In Rugby you need to focus your attention on the ball rather than the reaction of people watching on the sidelines. Many of the top sportspeople interviewed in David Hemery's book *The Pursuit of Sporting Excellence* rated concentration as a very important factor for them. A simple exercise to develop concentration is to sit, comfortable and relaxed in a chair, and to close your eyes. Then start counting each exhalation, starting at one and counting with each breath. You need to maintain a state of 'relaxed concentration' to get to the high numbers. Alternatively, why not try the balance exercises again? Now that you know what to concentrate on you should be more successful.

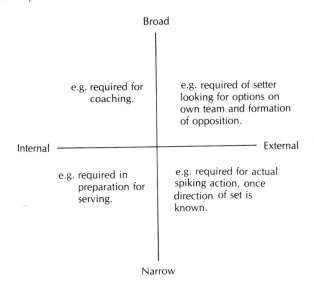

Fig 68   *Differing types of attention in Rugby.*

Focusing Your Attention

Part of sports concentration, as already suggested, is the ability to attend to the right things at the right time. Fig 68 illustrates the process of attention in sport and shows that attention is made up of at least two parts – direction and focus. The direction of attention is the internal–external line on the diagram and refers to the extent we attend to things internally (such as thoughts and feelings) or externally (objects in our environment). The other line in Fig 68 is the focus or width of attention (broad–narrow) and refers to whether our attention is narrowly focused (on the ball) or broadly focused (on the changing defensive pattern of the opposition). Four main types of attention can be deduced from Fig 68 and applied to different situations in Rugby.

The top left square is the broad–internal (analysis) style of attention required by the coach, who needs to be able to see things in a broad way – such as the way the entire team is functioning – but who at the same time focuses internally on his or her thoughts and feelings about the way the game is going, possible changes to be made at half-time and so on. The top right square is the broad–external (assessment) focus of attention often required by a fly-half in Rugby. For example, the fly-half not only has to adjust to the way the ball is fed to him or her (requiring an external focus), but must also be aware of the opposition tacklers and fellow three-quarters (broad focus).

The lower right square refers to the external–narrow (action) focus needed during the execution of a tactical kick. This is because the kicker, once committed to the kick, should focus on his or her own body movement and skill (narrow) as well as where the ball is to be placed (external). Finally, the lower left square is internal–narrow and is the focus of attention needed for the preparation of a skill. In Rugby this might occur just prior to kicking for goal when attention should be focused narrowly on the exact skill itself.

An American psychologist, Robert Nideffer, who devised the model in Fig 68, suggests that it is not enough just to adopt the right focus of attention at the right time, but that it is also critical to be able to *shift* attention from one square to the next as appropriate. Many people in sport are unable to do this effectively because they have a 'preferred style' and tend to stick to it. Clearly, this leads to errors in the game and Rugby players and coaches should work on attentional focus and this ability to shift attention. For example, after a score the player could shift to an internal–narrow focus in order to control tension, and then quickly shift to a broad–external style to see where other players are positioned. Further details on this subject can be found in Nideffer's mental training manual listed at the end of this book.

Self-Confidence

Self-confidence is one of the key areas of mental training for sport. It is very rare indeed for successful sportspeople to have a persistent lack of self-confidence. In understanding self-confidence, four main factors need to be identified. These are: prior performance; demonstration and imitation; verbal persuasion and positive self-talk; monitoring arousal. The most powerful source of confidence is likely to be your past performances and since success will lead to confidence and confidence to success, a 'positive-confidence cycle' can be set up. If your sports performance is improving then all is fine, but, what can you do when your performance is declining?

How can you break into the confidence cycle? One technique which has been shown to be effective is goal-setting (to be considered later in this chapter).

A second source of confidence is observation and imitation of others. Coaches can organise highly effective learning situations for Rugby players through the use of demonstrations, films and so forth which can act as confidence-building sessions. For example, a player lacking confidence in tackling may benefit from watching someone perform the skill successfully. (However, it is not always such a good idea constantly to show the 'ideal' skill executed by the best player as this may deflate confidence with players saying to themselves 'I'll never be able to do it like that!') Live and recorded demonstrations have been found to be effective, as well as techniques which physically assist players to adopt the correct positions. This is more usual in sports such as gymnastics but can be used for some Rugby skills (scrummaging, for example). In addition, players may build confidence through imagining correct skills, so highlighting again the importance of mental imagery.

A third source of confidence is verbal persuasion from others, although this may be a relatively weak source of confidence, depending upon the people involved; certainly encouragement from a highly respected person can help. A better source of persuasion is likely to come from within the player. Confidence-building statements are sometimes referred to as 'positive self-talk' or 'affirmations'. The most famous example in sport is Mohammed Ali's 'I am the greatest!' Although it may sound odd, there are plenty of examples of people gaining confidence from saying positive things to themselves. Three techniques for developing positive self-talk and affirmations are given in Fig 69.

Technique	Method	Comments
'As if' visualisation	Imagine you are someone or something which creates confidence for you. Example: imagine you are ten feet tall when jumping in the line-out.	You can add a positive slogan (*see* below) to go with this exercise.
Positive slogans	Think of a slogan which, when you see it, gives you confidence and direction.	Write it on a card and keep it in a prominent place.
Special words	Think of key or special words which are likely to help confidence, such as 'TIGHT' when scrummaging, or 'POWER' when running.	

Fig 69   Techniques for developing confidence through words and images (based on Syer and Connolly's Sporting Body, Sporting Mind*).*

A further source of self-confidence can be found in the physiological arousal of the body. If the stress response (referred to earlier) is thought to indicate negative feelings such as fear, then arousal will reduce confidence. The typical reaction here would be for a player, at a critical time in the game, to say, 'I can feel my heart pounding. Hell, I'm scared!' Conversely, if the player sees the reaction differently, it could become a positive influence. For example, he or she could say, 'I can feel my heart pounding. That's great! I'm ready for this!' Changing such negative thoughts into positive ones can be a useful confidence strategy.

Goal-Setting

One of the best ways to develop confidence and build sound psychological principles into your training is to use goal-setting. Although many people in sport use some kind of planning which approximates to the setting of goals, probably little thought has gone into the best ways of utilising goal-setting. Before outlining a simple goal-setting exercise for Rugby players, the following guidelines should be noted:

(i)   Goals can be set for the short-term, medium-term or long-term. To help immediate motivation and action, short-term goals are best.
(ii)   Goals should be specific and measurable. Just to set the goal of 'improving my line-out jumping' does not give enough direction. Set a goal that is highly specific and that can be measured for success. Feedback based on such measurements is crucial for successful goal-setting.
(iii)   Goals should be realistic, but challenging. It is easy to set very high goals, but disappointment will set in if they are not reached. On the other hand, very easy goals will not create extra motivation and direction.
(iv)   Goals should be accepted and worthwhile. For goals to be effective they must be accepted by the participant (hence it is best for the player to be involved in the goal-setting process rather than simply the coach), and considered worth the effort involved.

Fig 70 shows a goal-setting example for a Rugby player. Study this and then complete your own using the structure in Fig 71.

Long-term goal	Goals for next month	Goals and action for this week
(i) To be the number one prop in the club. (ii) To be selected for county team.	(i) To improve leg strength so that 3 × 6 reps back squat are achieved on 130kg.	(i) Two weight training sessions with 5 × 5 reps 80% front squat and back squat. (ii) 3 × 10 reps leg extensions with 50kg.

Fig 70   Examples of goal-setting in Rugby.

Long term goal	Goals for next month	Goals and action for this week
		(i) (ii)
		(i) (ii)
		(i) (ii)

Fig 71   Your goal-setting chart.

Team-Work

The final topic for mental training that will be considered here refers to team-work. There is no magic formula for getting teams to work well together, although some guidelines may help. Further details can be found in *Sporting Body, Sporting Mind* by Syer and Connolly.

Understanding Others

A key to effective team-work is understanding why other people are playing the game – it may come as a surprise that people do not play Rugby for the same reasons. Three main types of reasons have been identified in the past:

(i)   To play to win.
(ii)   To play well and demonstrate skill.
(iii) To be part of a team.

Clearly these reasons will exist in players to varying degrees and some may be interested in all three aspects. Nevertheless, coaches, team leaders and others may find that knowing their colleagues' main reasons for playing could help relationships within the team and between players and coaches. For example, the player wanting to demonstrate skills will be far less tolerant of being a reserve for a game than the person who is happy simply being a member of the squad.

Team Togetherness

It is often assumed that teams which are cohesive will play better. Although there have been exceptions, this is generally true. However, the cohesion of the team is not a simple matter; players have different personalities and will react differently in various situations. The group 'psych-up', therefore, is likely only to work for some of the players.

It is best to view group cohesion in two ways. Firstly, the extent to which players view the team as a whole (cohesion, togetherness, unity and so forth) and secondly, the degree of attraction the individual player has to the group. Both of these can have two 'orientations', or ways of working – task and social. A task orientation is where the focus is on getting the job done. This would mean that the team is primarily motivated to play well and to win, rather than to enjoy each other's company. A social orientation, on the other hand, is geared towards social relationships rather than group perform-ance. One would expect a social orientation to be stronger in more 'casual' teams and a task orientation to be stronger in high-level or professional teams, although there is no reason why most teams should not possess an interest in both orientations to some degree.

Team Meetings

John Syer and Christopher Connolly have identified three types of team meeting that may be useful in developing mental skills for teams:

(i)   Pre-game meetings. These are for the team to warm up in the emotional and psychological sense. They should be short, to the point and conducive to individual as well as team needs. You should bear in mind earlier discussions about the Rugby 'psych-up'.

(ii)   Post-game discussion meetings. These are held at the training session after a game to discuss the team's performance and to plan for the future. Group goal-setting can take place here.

(iii)   Team-spirit meetings. Numerous discussion topics may be aired although this meeting will probably not take place very often.

One aspect of mental training that should help the team effort is that if every player in the team makes a commitment to mental training, then this in itself should assist the cohesiveness and 'togetherness' of the team.

POSTSCRIPT

To restate the comments at the beginning of this chapter, mental training pro-vides a positive step forward towards becoming a more 'complete' Rugby player. Everyone will be doing it in the years to come, so why not get a 'head' start?

6 Summary and Programme Planning

In this book we have attempted to provide coverage of the major areas of training for Rugby. These are:

(i) Skill development.
(ii) Physical fitness.
(iii) Nutrition.
(iv) Injury prevention.
(v) Mental training.

Of course, it is not easy to fit all of these into the day-to-day training programme. However, each of these should form part of the regular ongoing training programme and two in particular – injury prevention and nutrition – should underpin each session rather than being a training session in its own right. So, having acquired this new-found wisdom, you will now need some guidelines for implementing the programme.

ASSESSMENT

A useful start is to assess your current level of training and performance. Only then can a proper 'prescription' and planning exercise take place. For example, assessment may show that you are relatively weak in arm strength and in the skill of two-hand catching in the line-out. These would then feature more extensively in your training programme. On a more general level, the training plan should follow the following structure:

(i) End of season recovery.
(ii) Preparation phase I (out of season).
(iii) Preparation phase II (pre-season).
(iv) Competition phase (the playing season).

The emphasis in each phase is shown in Figs 72 and 73. These outline no more than a basic plan and it is likely that different players will have to adapt this to meet their own needs. However, it is impossible to play at a peak for every game and so some priority must be placed on certain matches. This will require more of a build-up to the important matches, with the heavier training loads before some of the less important games. This might mean that the training reverts back to period 3 (preparation phase II in Fig 72) for a few

Training component	PERIOD 1	2	3	4
Mental training		★★	★★★	★★★
Aerobic training		★★★	★★	★★
Strength		★★★	★★	★★
Muscular endurance		★★★	★★	★★
Power		★	★★★	★★
Speed		★	★★	★★★
Flexibility		★★	★★	★
Individual skills		★★★	★★	★
Team skills		★	★★	★★★

Period 1   End of season recovery (up to 2 weeks).
Period 2   Preparatory phase I, out of season (June/July).
Period 3   Preparatory phase II, pre-season (August/September).
Period 4   Competition phase.

★★★ very important
 ★★ important
  ★ lower priority (maintenance)

Fig 72   Planning your training throughout the year (forwards).

Training component	PERIOD 1	2	3	4
Mental training		★★	★★★	★★★
Aerobic training		★★	★	★
Strength		★★★	★★	★
Muscular endurance		★★★	★★	★
Power		★	★★	★★★
Speed		★	★★	★★★
Flexibility		★★	★★	★★
Individual skills		★★	★★★	★★★
Team skills		★	★★	★★★

Period 1   End of season recovery (up to 2 weeks).
Period 2   Preparatory phase I, out of season (June/July).
Period 3   Preparatory phase II, pre-season (August/September).
Period 4   Competition phase.

★★★ very important
 ★★ important
  ★ lower priority (maintenance)

Fig 73   Planning your training throughout the year (three-quarters).

Level	Physical fitness	Skill training	Mental training
Beginner and club player.	Foundation principles – all components.	Basic individual techniques.	Relaxation, arousal control, goal-setting.
County and regional player.	Greater emphasis on individual needs and weaknesses.	Development of advanced skills.	Problem-solving skills.
National and international player.	Specialised intensive training.	Maintenance and development of individual skills, advanced group skills at speed.	Self-sufficiency in mental skills, advanced individualised techniques.

Fig 74   Training patterns for Rugby players of different levels.

weeks before period 4 (competition phase) is performed prior to the desired 'peak'. Do not try to stay with the training schedules of period 4 for too long as staleness or 'burn-out' may occur.

It is usual to change the pattern of training throughout the year to get the best results when required. This is called 'periodisation' or 'cycling' the training year by doing different exercises at different times. The main reasons for using periodisation are:

(i)   To vary the training load.
(ii) To aid recovery.
(iii) To achieve peak performance at a desired time.

This is particularly important for more advanced players who need to peak for specific matches, although beginners should also have variety in training.

A BALANCED PROGRAMME

A balanced training programme is important for all players. The game itself requires skill, fitness, mental skills, and many more qualities. This means that your training must also reflect such diverse needs. Fig 74 shows how the 'playing level' might affect the training.

CONCLUSION

It is to be hoped that you can now get closer to fulfilling your own goals of personal improvement and enjoyment through a higher standard of Rugby by implementing the training ideas from this book.

Glossary

Aerobic 'With oxygen'; used to describe 'steady-state' exercise where the body relies on oxygen as a continuous source of fuel.

Amenorrhoea Absence of normal female monthly cycle or periods.

Amino Acid The constituent parts of protein: eight of these acids cannot be made in the body (these are termed essential) and must form part of our diet. Another twelve can by synthesised in the body.

Anaemia A deficiency of red blood cells, or of their haemoglobin. Most likely to occur in women with heavy periods or otherwise due to insufficient iron replacement.

Anaerobic 'Without oxygen'; used to describe the energy systems of the body which are used in short, high-intensity exercise.

Basal Metabolic Rate (BMR) A term used to describe the absolute amount of energy required to maintain the body function for life. It is a very precise measure made when the subject is awake, at perfect rest, 12 hours after a meal and in a thermoneutral environment.

Body Mass Index (BMI) A convenient way to express the ratio of height to weight and give a simple estimate of abnormal weight for height. BMI is weight (kilograms) divided by the height (metres) squared and should lie in the range 17–25.

Caffeine A drug found in tea, coffee, chocolate and some carbonated beverages. Promotes fatty acid release, affects the cardiovascular system and is a diuretic.

Calorie A very small, precisely defined unit of heat. One thousand calories are equivalent to one kilocalorie or kcal.

Carbohydrates Molecules containing carbon, hydrogen and oxygen. They may be small simple units, often sweet, such as glucose, sucrose or larger units, often tasteless, such as starch. We cannot digest all carbohydrates and some are termed 'unavailable'; these include cellulose (dietary fibre). Carbohydrates provide energy for the body, about 4kcals per gram or 120kcals per ounce.

Cardiorespiratory Exercise
Exercise such as running, cycling, swimming, or any exercise utilising large muscle groups for an extended period of time; develops the ability of the blood, heart, lungs and other systems of the body to persist in work.

Cool-Down A period of light exercise and stretching after vigorous activity.

Dehydration Loss of body fluid with inadequate replacement. Liable to result from excessive sweating, diarrhoea or vomiting.

Dietary Deficiency Inadequate intake of an essential nutrient which results in reduced body stores of the nutrient and eventually affects body function. Diagnosis of a deficiency requires biochemical tests.

Dietary Fibre That part of our food which is not digested by our normal digestive juices and therefore remains in the intestine providing bulk. However, dietary fibre is largely digested by organisms in the large bowel and as such can be absorbed to provide energy.

Dislocation A displacement of the bony surfaces at a joint so that the ends of the bones do not meet, or meet incorrectly. Requires immediate referral to a doctor.

Doping The use of substances which artificially improve or augment an athlete's performance.

Fats Molecules containing carbon, hydrogen and oxygen. The small molecules are called fatty acids and dietary fats are a mixture of different fatty acids often held together by another molecule of glycerol and are then referred to simply as fat. Fats provide energy, 9kcals per gram or 270kcals per ounce.

Glycogen The form in which the mammalian body stores carbohydrate. It is mainly stored in the liver and muscles and constitutes a very mobile but limited store of energy for the body. It can be used without the presence of oxygen, i.e. anaerobically.

Grid An area of playing-field or playground subdivided into equal-sized squares for skills practices or small-sided games.

Grubber Kick A kick which propels the ball along the ground, using either the instep or the top of the foot.

Haemoglobin The oxygen-carrying component of red blood cells composed of an iron-based substance.

Isokinetic A form of resistance training where a machine provides resistance which allows for constant limb speed.

Isometric A form of resistance training where no movement takes place.

Isotonic A form of resistance training involving the lifting of free-standing objects, such as barbells.

Joule A very small and precise measure of the amount of work. The energy in food is related to the amount of work it can generate and therefore sometimes the energy value of food is expressed in joules. One thousand joules form one kilojoule or kJ. One kcal is equivalent to 4.2kJ.

Ligaments Strong bands of fibrous tissue which bind bones together at a joint.

Loop This occurs when one player runs behind another in order to take up a position to receive a pass – often used to create an overlap in attack.

Maul This is formed by one or more players from each team, who, on their feet and in physical contact, close round a player in possession of the ball.

Mental Imagery The process of practising a skill in your mind rather than through physical practice.

Minerals Inert substances some of which are essential to the body for its functioning. Calcium, magnesium, sodium, potassium, phosphorus, iron and zinc are some of these essential minerals.

Miss Pass A long pass which misses out the next player, who would normally receive the ball.

Muscular Endurance The ability to contract a muscle, or group of muscles, over time.

Nutrients Those parts of food which are used by the body to allow functioning of cells. Carbohydrates and fats are 'burned' to provide energy for cells to work – internally in order to make more tissue, for example, and externally to propel the body. Protein, vitamins and minerals are all used by the cells to function normally.

Osteoarthritis The surfaces of bones at a joint are covered in cartilage which may become worn away, particularly in a joint which has been previously damaged. The joint may be painful, swollen and stiff. This condition is osteoarthritis.

Osteoporosis A condition, mainly in women, in which the bones become increasingly thin and brittle – it is caused by reduced sex hormones and possibly low intake of calcium.

Overload System in which training is progressively increased.

Power The combination of strength and speed.

Progressive Muscle Relaxation (PMR) A form of relaxation training which teaches the recognition of tension and relaxation through a series of muscle-tension exercises.

Proprioceptive Neuromusclar Facilitation (PNF) A form of flexibility training which requires the muscle to be contracted before stretching.

Protein That part of the food which contains amino acids. It can be used for energy and provides 4kcals per gram or 120kcals per ounce.

Reaction Time The time which elapses between the stimulus and the start of the movement in response to the stimulus.

Ruck This is formed when the ball is on the ground and one or more players from each team are on their feet and in physical contact – with the ball between them.

Scissors or Switch Pass This occurs when the receiver runs in the opposite (attacking) direction to the ball carrier, taking a short pass and so changing the direction of attack.

Screen Pass The ball carrier uses his body to screen the ball from the opposition while holding the ball out for a supporting player – who cuts close and drives past the opposition.

Shuttle Practices High-intensity practices in which groups of players move back and forth between two lines. These are used for repetition-passing practices with a number of players in a small area (perhaps across a grid).

Skinfold Thickness The layer of body fat which lies directly beneath the skin which can be measured using skinfold callipers. This layer of fat is related to total body fat and it is possible to estimate total body fat from this method.

Sorbothane A synthetic substance which absorbs energy well and is used as a 'shock-absorber' for inserts into shoes, mainly at the heel.

Sports Anaemia Probably not a true anaemia; the increase in plasma volume brought on by a serious training schedule dilutes the red cells reducing their concentration, the total number of red cells remaining the same.

Sprain An injury to the ligaments around a joint which may produce pain, swelling and discolouration.

Strength The ability of the muscle to exert force.

Stress Fracture A minute crack in a bone due to repeated overloading by an inappropriately rapid increase in training loads.

Tendon White 'cords' which attach muscles to bones. They may become inflamed (tendonitis), partially torn, or completely broken (ruptured tendon).

Tonicity of Fluid The concentration of particles in a solution compared to the concentration of particles in body fluids, especially blood. If the concentration in a solution is greater than blood it is termed hypertonic; if lower in concentration, hypotonic. Water will always travel from a less concentrated solution to a more concentrated solution.

Variable Resistance Training A form of resistance training which varies the loading to accommodate the mechanical efficiency of the body levers so that optimal tension is placed on the muscle throughout the whole range of movement.

Vitamins Molecules which are found in food and are essential to cells for their efficient functioning. Some vitamins are associated and soluble in fat (vitamins A, D, E, K), others are soluble in water (Vitamins B and C).

Warm-Up Light, mainly aerobic and flexibility exercises prior to vigorous activity.

Further Reading

Game Skills

Corless, B., *Rugby Union* (The Crowood Press, 1985)*
Greenwood, J., *Total Rugby: 15-man Rugby for Coaches and Players* (A & C Black, 1985)*

Physical and Mental Fitness

Alter, M., *The Science of Stretching* (Human Kinetics, 1988)
Fleck, S. and Kraemer, W., *Designing Resistance Training Programmes* (Human Kinetics, 1987)*
Fox, E., *Sports Physiology* (Saunders College, 1979)
Hazeldine, R., *Fitness for Sport* (The Crowood Press, 1985)*
Hemery, D., *The Pursuit of Sporting Excellence* (Collins Willow, 1986)
Lear, P.J., *Weight Training: Know the Game* (A & C Black, 1988)
National Coaching Foundation, *Physiology and Performance* (1986)
National Coaching Foundation, *The Coach at Work* (1986)
National Strength and Conditioning Association Journal
Nideffer, R.M., *The Athlete's Guide to Mental Training* (Human Kinetics 1985)
Railo, W., *Willing to Win* (Springfield Books, 1986)
Syer, J. and Connolly, C., *Sporting Body, Sporting Mind* (Cambridge Univesity Press, 1984)*
Terry, P., *The Winning Mind* (Thorsons, 1989)*

Nutrition

DHSS, *Recommended Amounts of Food Energy and Nutrients for Groups of People in the UK* (Report on Health and Social Subjects No. 15, 1979)
Eisenmann, P. and Johnson D., *Coaches' Guide to Nutrition and Weight Control* (Human Kinetics, 1982)
Haskell, W. *et al.*, *Nutrition and Athletic Performance* (Bull Publishing, 1982)
Ministry of Agriculture, Fisheries and Food, *Manual of Nutrition* (HMSO, 1985)
Paul, A. and Southgate, D., *McCance and Widdowson's 'The Composition of Foods'* (HMSO, 1978)

Sports Injuries

Anderson, B., *Stretching* (Pelham, 1980)
Grisogono, V., *Sports Injuries: a Self-Help Guide* (John Murray, 1984)*
National Coaching Foundation, *Safety First for Coaches* (1986)
Read, M. and Wade P., *Sports and Medicine* (Butterworth, 1981)
St John Ambulance, *First Aid Manual* (Dorling Kindersley, 1982)

*particularly recommended

Useful Addresses

British Amateur Weight Lifters' Association, 3, Iffley Turn, Oxford OX4 4DY.
British Association of Sports Sciences, c/o National Coaching Foundation (*see* below).
National Coaching Foundation, 4, College Close, Beckett Park, Leeds LS6 3QH.
National Strength & Conditioning Association, P.O. Box 81410, Lincoln, Nebraska 68501, USA.

RFU Divisional Offices:
London:
   North East London Polytechnic, Longbridge Road, Dagenham, Essex RM8 2AS.
Midlands:
   c/o James Gilberts, 5, St Matthew's Street, Rugby, Warwickshire.
North:
   Leeds International Pool, Westgate, Leeds LS1 4PH.
South West:
   Taunton School, Staplegrove Road, Taunton, Somerset.
Rugby Football Union (headquarters), Whitton Road, Twickenham TW1 1DZ.

Sports Council, 16, Upper Woburn Place, London WC1H 0QP.
St John Ambulance, Supplies Department, Priory House, St John's Gate, Clerkenwell, London EC1M 4DA.

Index